Praise for

Love Me as I Am

"Poignant, candid. . . . An inspirational memoir that fans
of the *Real Housewives* franchise or *The Real* will enjoy . . .
And yes: she dishes about the other housewives and the
celebrities she met on her road to success."

—*Library Journal*

"Dishy, warm, and entertaining."

—*Kirkus Reviews*

Love Me as I Am

Also by Garcelle Beauvais

I Am Mixed

I Am Living in 2 Homes

I Am Awesome

Garcelle Beauvais

WITH NICOLE E. SMITH

Love Me as I Am

AMISTAD
An Imprint of HarperCollins*Publishers*

HarperCollins books may be purchased for educational, business, or sales promotional use. For information, please email the Special Markets Department at SPsales@harpercollins.com.

FIRST HARPERCOLLINS PAPERBACK PUBLISHED IN 2023

Designed by Leah Carlson-Stanisic

*Art by Suns07butterfly/Shutterstock, Inc.,
Niki Paronak/Shutterstock, Inc., Le Panda/Shutterstock, Inc., and
Anastasia Lembrrik/Shutterstock, Inc*

Library of Congress Cataloging-in-Publication Data
is available upon request.

ISBN 978-0-06-309959-3

23 24 25 26 27 LBC 5 4 3 2 1

This book is dedicated to my mother, Marie Claire Beauvais; KeKe. You gave me the wings to fly and the freedom to be unconventionally fearless in my journey. You will always be the beautiful butterfly on my shoulder.

I also dedicate this book to my three boys, Oliver, Jax, and Jaid. You have taught me how to love, forgive, and keep pushing past my pain. You gave me purpose and balance. Thank you for sharing your mommy with the world.

There is only one way to avoid criticism:

do nothing, say nothing, and be nothing.

—Aristotle

Contents

Prologue

This book is about my journey to finding Garcelle . . . finding my G-spot. Initially, many of you might think that this will be just a salacious collection of sexually charged kiss-and-tell stories from my life. Not my intention, but I hope you won't be disappointed. Wink. Wink. To me, the tongue-in-cheek phrase G-spot means my core. Translated, it means digging deep and dealing head on with principles I still struggle to wrap my mind around. It means finding contentment and peace even in my weakest, darkest, and most lonely moments. When there're no lights, camera, and even when I'm getting *no* action. Yes, that's the real G-spot for me. The understanding and acceptance of the many bits and parts that make up my truths.

Keeping it real is at the center of my truth. Keeping it real with myself, my colleagues, my family, and my friends. It's not in my nature to fake it. The truth is always written all over my face and flowing from my soul. Some can handle it and others can't. I can't change other people; I can only make sure that I stay faithfully committed to showing up authentically. So that I show up like the best version of Garcelle.

Getting to the core of my best self and shining light, this is where I continue to find my greatest satisfaction and release. By getting up every morning; giving life everything I've got, so I can try to perfect me and share the best version of myself with my kids, family, and friends.

One

Childhood

Childhood is the most
beautiful of all
life's lessons.

—Rachel Carson

With a unique name such as Garcelle, you would have to expect that my life would be colorful and unconventional. How a little Black girl, with an absentee father, from a small island in the Caribbean had the audacity to dream of being an international model, actress, author, producer, and reinventor of herself I will never begin to know. God is great!

Marie Claire Beauvais brought me into the world on a Monday morning under a full moon on November 28, 1966. To let you in on a little secret, I actually celebrate two birthdays. Even though I was born on the twenty-eighth, when they were doing my immigration paperwork at the airport when immigrating to the United States, the twenty-sixth was mistakenly recorded . . . fun fact!

My father's name was Axel Jean-Pierre. Rumor has it, he left to get milk or ice cream when I was three or four years old. I didn't see him again until I was fourteen. And I've never looked at the ice cream man the same way ever again. Poof! Just like that he vanished into thin air. I guess he either never found the ice cream, or just forgot our address. I was way too young to remember the exact details of the day it happened, but definitely not too nosey to snoop around and eavesdrop on the adult whispering about it. I was also very aware and had a front row seat to see the tears of sadness that welled up in my mom's eyes for years after he left. I believe he was the love of her life—I think I overheard that too—and his betrayal left a huge gash on her heart and mine too.

Either way, I don't remember much of anything about him during my early years. I don't have memories of us snuggling or me sitting on his lap and being held. I don't have a distinctive smell of cologne or tender moment to associate with him. I have no fond stories of warm tender hugs or soothing bedtime stories before I drifted off to sleep. No words of wisdom or fatherly advice on boys and men to lament on. There was no paternal bond or air of familiarity and affection with this person who I was told was my dad. The word "dad" for me at a young age held no meaning or customary feelings of safety, protection, or love to associate with it. He simply didn't exist, and my world consisted of just me, my mom, my sisters, brothers, and some extended family.

I was the youngest of seven children. Three older siblings—Maurice, Yves-Rose, and Carole—all had the same father. Then came my sisters Gladys, Chantal, and my brother Elie, who had another father. They happened to grow up in Montreal, Canada, with their father. Then there was me, whom my mother had with my father, Axel Jean-Pierre. I never took his last name and I ended up with my mother's maiden name instead.

I was a Peenie Greet, or skinny twig, as my brother Maurice referred to me. I was painfully skinny, a little on the taller side, and lacking the hint of curves that many young Haitian women inherit from their mothers and grandmothers. We Haitians l-o-v-e our nicknames! I was so skinny that my older sister Carole, who loved sewing and making dresses, would call on me when she needed a ruler. She would tell me to lie down and then use my legs like a big stencil to trace out fabric lengths. Desperate to gain some weight, I would eat and immediately lay down, hoping that the food would settle and miraculously stick to my bones, creating extra curves. I hated my protruding "wings" on my back, as I called them. I agonized that I looked like I was going to fly away in the wind because my shoulder blades stuck out so much. Oh, and because they made me feel self-conscious, I hated wearing halter tops. What I wouldn't do to go back and tell that little girl that those lovely bones and never-ending twig-like legs would be her blessings instead of her curses in life.

I was never given a middle name. Instead, I embraced my

nickname, not the Peenie Greet one, but the name Gachou. I whole-heartedly loved this pet name, but I'm not totally convinced it even had a real meaning or an official way to spell it. I think it represents a mashup of my name somewhere in there with a little extra umph and love. Looking back now I think I loved the name Gachou because it made me feel loved and instantly defined me culturally. It still does. If you didn't have a nickname you simply weren't Haitian, so I wear it proudly. Until this day Gachou is who I am to my family, and even to my close friends.

Port-au-Prince, where I spent my earliest years, was the capital city of Haiti. My neighborhood was in a somewhat middle-class setting. It was a small, simple, and rustic existence. When I say my mom was middle class, I mean that we weren't extremely poor, especially according to Haitian standards, but we were far from being rich. Nothing flashy or extravagant. Small backwoods red clay roads well traveled by goats, sheep, and donkeys. I remember there was always a sweet smell of freshness in the air that would greet you as you stepped out of the house. The warm rays of the sun always greeted you and wrapped you in a cloak of happiness. I used to love to squint into the sun until my eyes would water and then blindly walk around feeling my way to familiarity. My mom would oil my hair and do it up in one or two pigtails with bright yellow ribbons, depending on her mood. It made me feel special, beautiful, and loved.

Majestically fragrant hibiscus and birds of paradise often lined pathways and created a visual landscape much like a living art gallery. While I walked to and from school accompanied by my caretaker, I would count the flowers while eating fresh tangerines. Ahh, the smell of fresh tangerines still brings back such warm memories. My mom would tell me that I would happily skip and dance carefree along the pathway in my bright blue plaid school uniform. It may sound idyllic, especially in contrast to the backdrop of the harsh realities of Haiti during that time, but I was way too young to digest the concepts of poverty and despair, and my time living there was very brief. One thing I can confirm is that I was never exposed to the social stigma assigned to people living in conditions of lack. In my childlike mind, some people lived in houses and some people lived in huts, but everyone was still part of my community, which I loved.

Everything seemed so bright, vibrant, and beautiful. Like many other island cultures, mine was full of bold expressions. Splashes of cheerful color were everywhere. From the most ramshackle roadside dwellings where clothing hung from makeshift clotheslines to the most palatial homes in Pétion-Ville, our culture had a deep appreciation for living life out loud. There's one thing about Haitians, we love color. Perhaps adding these joyful "hues of hope" changed my people's overall outlook on daily life. If someone was to tell me that the concept of color therapy was created in these islands, I'd believe them. Even now, bold colors are more than a visual thing, they are a reflection of an attitude.

Merchants lined the city streets for blocks selling fresh produce and other handcrafted goods under colorful canopies. Mangoes, sugarcane, melons, pineapples, bananas, and kenep were the fruits of my youth. Walking down the road, you would always make it a point to greet your elders with *bonjour* (in the morning) or *bonsoir* (in the evening) because showing respect, even for strangers, was important. I remember marveling at the strong women who would walk around perfectly erect balancing huge wicker baskets of produce and other items on their heads. Looking up at them with their overflowing baskets made them seem like towering giants. How did they carry so much and make it look so effortless? Isn't this the question we usually ask when we talk about a woman's burdens?

Even though civil unrest and poverty were forces crippling the island during my early years in Haiti, everyone always seemed happy, grateful, and genuinely joyful to be alive. They radiated the same colors we saw everywhere. Local expressions of art were constants in every corner of the island. Colorful artwork depicting women and men at work, at play, and at rest boldly announced that my people were not only talented, they were also hopeful and proud. Even public buses, or tap-taps as they're called, were painted with eye-catching scenes of hardworking Haitians toiling in the vein of our culture. I've been drawn to this type of cultural art, even to this day. It brings me comfort, joy, and pride. It's a symbol of home, and I connect with it on a soulful level. Haitian art is always prominently featured throughout my home. I want my kids to also develop an appreciation for it and remember what they're made of.

Just as my country's vividly bold color was to the eyes, music was to the ears. Compas music was the soundtrack of my youth. I remember the infectious sound of rhythmic beats from handcrafted tanbou drums, guitars, and tcha-tchas shaking while people moved their hips in anticipation of the next beat. It was simply trance-inducing. I remember hearing the beating drums at night and my mom shooing us inside because they were the drums of a voodoo ceremony. I remember feeling a bit of fear. I am not sure why. Voodoo was very much a part of every Haitian's life. Either because you practiced it, or simply because you revered it for its mysterious power and fabled legacy. My family, I believe, was in the latter category.

The tempo of animated Creole was also another soothingly recognizable sound that rang throughout the air. It's a language overflowing with full-throated exuberant inflections and singsong types of chimes. People everywhere had so much to say. Things to say in laughter and jest. Things to say in anger and frustration. I came from a stock of people who did not hold their tongues and always shared what was on their mind. Whether you liked it or not! I remember sitting around eavesdropping on adult conversations. To the outside world, these exchanges might have sounded like heated arguments, but to me, it was just normal chatter. It was comforting. The type of French Creole spoken in Haiti was born out of a combination of West African languages synthesized by our ancestors who were enslaved. Creole has its roots in European French, with a whole lot of African seasoning, just like my people, who give it life.

Looking back, I could tell that there was a stark visual difference in my house compared to others, but it never translated to our family's value or worth. My mother was a trained nurse and was able to provide a decent living for us. In the early years, I remember that we had a helper in the house. Our helper cooked, cleaned, and took care of me, since my mother was a single mom. Even though my mother employed helpers, I was never raised to believe that they were there to "serve" me. They were there to help my mom do the things she didn't have time to do. And when she wasn't there to look after me, they were like surrogate parents who I'd better obey. Believe me, if Sawrelia told my mother I had misbehaved, the punishment would have been just the same as if my mother had been there to see it herself.

One of my most cherished memories from the early years growing up in Haiti was of visiting my maternal grandmother, Mamacici, in the country village of St. Marc. It was a central city in Haiti and the place of my actual birth. Mamacici had a big, sprawling house with a storefront below that she owned and operated. I always remember running down the dirt road to her house and coming up over the bridge and seeing her big home. I loved her house and I loved her even more. Clear jars of brightly colored candy and sweets (surette) were always lined up and ready for purchase by the neighborhood residents. She was just as sweet as the candy she sold. I never would have believed she carried around such sadness, but she did. She always seemed so strong and happy. My mom's father, Papa Maurice, left her and my grandmother so he could be with a younger woman. He started another family and stayed with them until he died. PUT A PIN IN THAT ONE . . . I'M SENSING A PATTERN!

Deep within me, the scared, confused, and oftentimes lonely, little, underweight Peenie Greet that I was, there was a fire ignited.

It was a fire you couldn't quantify. A fire you couldn't easily extinguish. I had seen so much happiness and deep sorrow from such an early age. I was, and have always been, full of questions about life and things that happened, but that doesn't mean I ever got any answers. I always wanted to know *how* and *why*, even more than I wanted to know *what*. Culturally, children were seen and not heard, but that didn't stop the questions from formulating in my head. It only stopped them from falling out of my lips. Frustrating yes, but I was innocently nurturing my insatiable curiosity streak and probably promising myself that once I could ask, I would ask everyone everything! Big-mouthed, opinionated children who asked a lot of questions were not welcome in my household. We just did what we were told and observed how things were done.

Even as a grown woman, my biggest regret is that I never asked my mother more questions before she died in 2008. I will never truly know what Marie Claire Beauvais, my mother, was thinking during those lonely nights right after my dad left. I'm sure she stayed up endlessly waiting for him to come home and cried herself to sleep. How do I know this? Because I've done it myself in my own life. There's that pattern again. What I do know is that she was never bitter. Never hateful, or vengeful, and always there providing for us. In her quiet and dignified way, she taught me the powerful lessons of fortitude and self-perseverance. Dealing with her own pain in the way she chose informed my narrative about being a woman and dealing with the loss of love.

Much like many immigrant stories, my mother briefly left me in

Haiti at six and set out in search of a better life on American soil. She had relatives in Boston who had already made the pilgrimage before her, and she felt her time had come to do the same. With very few options, I was left in the care of my older siblings Yves-Rose and Carole during the time she went to figure out our transition.

My sisters became like my mother, and they took good care of me. I'm sure if I dwell on these circumstances too much it might induce feelings of buried trauma. Putting myself, or even my own children, in the shoes of that little six-year-old girl, I can only imagine it was heart-wrenching and scary to have your mom leave you. I can't say I didn't internalize that pain, or suffer any long-standing effects because of it.

Putting on my hat as a mother, I can't imagine doing that to my kids at age six. On the flip side, I also can't imagine living in circumstances where I truly believed that leaving my home would be my only option for prosperity either. America was portrayed as the land of milk and honey for many people outside its borders. It was a beacon of hope, success, and prosperity that everyone wanted a piece of. A good mother will move heaven and earth to give her children what she thinks they need. The courage it must have taken. The guilt and fear my mom must have felt. Not only fear for us and our well-being, but also fear and uncertainty for conquering a new world. Knowing my mother, she knew I was in good hands with my older siblings and my caretaker, and that gave her comfort. In her absence, my older sisters Yves-Rose and Carole taught me a great deal and stepped in to fill that void when I needed them the most. They put the word "family" into practice and exemplified the meaning of "it takes a village."

Hello Peabody, Massachusetts . . . what a rude awakening! About a year and a half after my mother left me in Haiti, she decided the time was right for all of us to move to the United States. She took a leap of faith and sent for me and my sisters, hoping for a fresh start. Correction—a cold start! My three middle siblings were already feeling winter's hell because they lived in Montreal, Canada, with their dad.

We landed in Boston during the dead of winter. There were mounds of blinding white snow everywhere. Everywhere it looked like the pictures I had seen of Christmas. Gone were the brightly colored fragrant flowers and the swaying palm trees. In their place, dirty, slippery snow and dripping icicles. It was unbearably freezing. If you know anything about Boston you know that cold is never just cold. During the first few days, I thought I had gained magical powers because I could see smoke coming out of my mouth whenever it opened. The magic faded pretty quickly when I realized that attached to this magically white wonderland were fingers and toes that were so painfully frozen, I thought I would die. My cute ponytails that I loved so much would freeze like ice cubes if they weren't fully dried after washing my hair. This actually felt like hell compared to the tropical, warm paradise life I had just left.

Another huge issue: I spoke Creole and French. I didn't speak a lick of English—not one drop! This made me feel very nervous and shy at first because people would look at me and say something, and I would look back with a blank stare, blinking endlessly. I knew they were talking to me because they were looking right at me and moving their lips, but there was absolutely no comprehension. Completely white noise. I was a smart child in Haiti, so my mother told me. Because I didn't speak the language when I arrived in Boston, I wasn't able to attend school right away. It was the 1970s, and public schools weren't set up to nurture and support new immigrant students and their families. I taught myself English by watching *Sesame Street* religiously. Try teaching a little immigrant girl, who didn't speak a drop of English, how to spell Massachusetts! Thank God for Big Bird and the Count . . . they really had my back.

The America, and more specifically Peabody, Massachusetts, in the 1970s that this little brown-skinned Haitian girl landed in was neither a kind nor a familiar one. Diversity was not a priority or on the radar of my town. As a child, I didn't realize the inner strength I was building but, as an adult, I am grateful for my journey and the toughness I found through it.

I remember being the only Black girl in my entire school. Think about that for a minute. There were no other kids that looked like me at all. Going from an environment where everyone in my school looked like me and spoke like me to an all-white school was instant culture shock. For a kid who was already shy this was the worst position to be in. I stood out like a sore thumb. To say that

Massachusetts was slow to embrace cultural differences is putting it mildly.

Once I started school, I loved it despite being different. I remember being so excited to start my new adventure and go to school on the first day. What I also remember is that adults and kids kept touching my skin and feeling my hair because they had never seen anything like them up close and personal. Despite the rough initiation, I assimilated well and began to make friends easily. I also enjoyed my usual milestone achievements, such as my First Communion. Mine was a pretty typical Catholic schoolgirl childhood. During my junior high and high school, I even gained enough confidence to become very active in the student council and joined almost every after-school club there was. I would sing, dance, and cheer louder and harder than anyone else. I loved being a cheerleader because I could be expressive and dramatic. I could yell, scream, jump around, and act crazy, all things I couldn't do at home. This was a great way to release some pent-up energy and teenage angst. I also loved the energy you would feel from the crowds and the encouragement they gave when we performed. It was magical.

Ignited by my love for cheering, I was developing a love of performing in general. I did every form of dance imaginable—jazz, ballet, tap, and any other class my mother could find. It married my two passions: music and moving my body to a beat. I would mastermind little plays and performances and coax my friends into participating. Yes, of course, I was always the lead and directing everyone into position and keeping them all on cue. I would excitedly gather my family around and sandwich them into our small living room to watch us perform. After a few awkwardly coordinated two-step sequences, shimmies, and some flamboyant twirls for good measure, we would take our final bows. We even had the audacity to request donations afterward. I distinctly remember my brother would only throw pennies at us after all our "hard work." Even then, I knew my talents were being completely undervalued. What a cheapskate!

My mother loved music too, causing me to love and dread the weekends equally because she would blast music and dance around all day long as she cooked and cleaned. At the time, it was even a little too much for me. Classical, reggae, jazz, merengue, compas—you name it, she played it. Religion, and going to church, was still a big part of our lives. Every Sunday, my mom would make sure we wore our Sunday best and religiously shuttle us off to church. Reflecting on my youth now as a grown woman, I see how the love of music my mom instilled in me has taken root. Music is all around me whenever I'm at home. It's like another part of the family.

The challenges of fitting in were not only happening outside of our home. My mother, who was a very proud Haitian woman, had a hard time loosening the reins so we could fully adapt to the new American way of life. Whenever she saw us doing or saying something that wasn't "typically Haitian," she would yell "Remember you're not American, you're Haitian!" This was such a confusing concept because as far as I saw it, I was here in America.

As I got a bit older, I would defiantly respond by saying, "If you didn't want us to be like Americans, why did you even bring us here?" Even though I was responding logically, I never listened to the unspoken meaning behind her words. I now understand that her statements had nothing to do with logic. They were uttered based on an internal fear that she was battling in her mind. It was a fear that must have made her constantly second-guess her immigration from her homeland. She feared we'd fall so much in love with American ways that we would forget everything about who we were and where we came from. That we would slowly lose our foundational roots. To her, it must have felt like we were in danger of losing our souls.

You see, that's the love-hate relationship that many first-generation immigrants have with the process of assimilation. We are never running from the richness of our culture; we are running toward the hope of new perceived opportunities.

I credit my trips to Dorchester, Massachusetts, to visit my cousins with giving me a love and appreciation for R & B music. To this day, it's my favorite and it speaks to my soul. Living in Peabody's mostly white community, I was never exposed to many Black people or Black culture. When I first met my cousins, I quickly realized that they were born in Colombia and only spoke Spanish, and I only spoke Creole French and very little English at the time. So what did we do? We would play, and there would be very few words spoken, but we still had a blast. Even though being skinny didn't bother me as much anymore, I remember always being envious of my cousin, Josanne, who looked like Thelma from the show *Good Times*. God, I wanted to have a shape like hers! All the guys would adoringly flutter around her and give her all the attention. She had big, beautiful curves in all the right places—all the things I never had. I just loved being next to her and basking in the glow from her admirers.

I couldn't get enough of my trips to see my cousins. We would hang out on the stoop listening to the latest music on our boom box. We loved taking note of the people walking by going about their daily errands. I loved, loved, loved seeing all the Black faces and smiles—they were electric, and it reminded me of living in Haiti. It was like looking into a mirror all the time. They made me feel warm and at home. I treasured seeing how my cousins acted and interacted with each other and their friends. To me, they acted just like the American kids did, and I was in awe. It was all new and very different from the Haitian culture because these American kids were allowed to be a little loud and rowdy and inwardly I loved it. When we would venture out to Boston, I would see Black people working in stores and behind desks. It was positively mind-blowing. I couldn't explain the difference, Boston was just different from Peabody, where I lived. Just more relaxed, familiar, and more welcoming. These times visiting my cousins and venturing out of our bubble were transformative for me.

My mom and I were very, very close. She was affectionate, but not overly affectionate. Her way of showing love was to buy me little things. Marie Claire—KeKe, as everyone called her—was an old school "girlie girl." She loved to dress up and smell nice. She always put herself together and fixed herself up with colorful clothes and her hair was always *done*. She was a strong woman who took great pride in her appearance and showed me how to do the same. I would beg her for these cute pink plastic kitten heel slippers that I loved. She would buy them and I'd wear them constantly. Actually, I would love them right into the ground and they'd break and I would be a wreck. She would give in and buy me a new pair and the cycle would start all over again. I guess that's how my shoe fetish started. A beautiful pair of shoes are my Achilles' heel even until this day. I loved playing dress up in her closet, trying on her beautiful sparkly, colorful clothes, pretending to be all grown up with important places to go!

My brother Maurice was the first to leave home. He chose to fully embrace American culture and enlist in the army. My mom was taking classes to learn how to teach and care for kids with disabilities. She was also a nurse who worked the 3:00 p.m. to 11:00 p.m. shift, which made me a proud latchkey kid. I would come home from school and I'd let myself in, or I would stay at home by myself until everybody else came home. Either my sisters would cook, or my mom would cook before she left and leave it on the stove. There were no sitters and helpers; we all pitched in and did our part to make the household run. At some point, my mom started dating a man named Kwaku, not sure how he spelled it. I remember him being a huge, sturdy man who seemed nice enough until that one questionable day.

One day, I got home from school early and let myself into the house. My mom hadn't made it home yet. As I entered the front door, I realized that I wasn't alone because Kwaku was there too. I guess he had his own key. Not only was he there, I remember he was in the bathroom because I heard the shower running. Initially, I didn't think anything of it. I nonchalantly made my way to the kitchen and made myself a snack, as was my normal routine. As I was taking my food back to my bedroom, I heard the door to the hallway bathroom slowly begin to creak open. It caused me to slow my stride because I was preparing to say a cordial hello to Kwaku. To my shock and horror, when the door fully opened, I saw him standing there completely naked! I mean not a stich of clothing to be found anywhere on him. The only thing he was wearing was a really weird smile, which made me super uncomfortable. For a split second, I was frozen in place because I'd never seen a naked man before. When I snapped out of it, I ran into my room, slammed the door, and locked it tightly behind me. I also made a point of sliding my dresser over to barricade myself in. The next day, when I finally saw my mom, I told her about the incident. I can't recall exactly how the exchange between us went, but what I do remember is that the next day she broke up with Kwaku and I never laid eyes on him again.

My mother was very protective of me. I wasn't allowed to have sleepovers at friends' homes. Even when it came to other family members, she never allowed me to sleep over at anyone's house if she wasn't there too. Looking back now, I think she was acutely aware of the unspeakable things that could happen to a young girl even at the hands of those closest to you. Perhaps she had experienced something traumatic in her own youth that caused her to be leery. I can't say for sure, but I do know that sleepovers were her redline that she didn't cross. Ever!

When I turned sixteen, my mom decided to ditch Boston for

warmer surroundings and moved us to Miami, Florida. During the time of our big relocation, I had a huge dance recital coming up that would have been thrown into disarray because of the shift. Remarkably, she let me stay behind with my dance teacher so I could do this recital and finish off my time in Boston, going out in a blaze of glory.

Now, this was living! This geographical move made more sense to me. I instantly took to the familiar warmth, vibrant colors, and palm trees. I was also super excited to go to a more diverse school again where kids looked like me, had hair like me, and shared similar cultures. Or so I thought. At the time, she had other family members living there too. Initially, I was enrolled into Norland Senior High School in Miami. When I got to the school, my transition wasn't all roses and lollipops, as I had imagined. I stood out because I was the new tall girl, but also because I apparently spoke proper English, or like "a white girl," as the kids coined it. Instantly the girls hated me and constantly threatened to beat me up after school. According to them, I didn't fit in because they said I thought I was white. Imagine the irony. Me, a little brown girl from Haiti who loved her Blackness "apparently" thought she was white . . . go figure. This was another dose of culture shock and a real head-scratcher for me. My mom, on the other hand, saw that there were a lot of girls popping up pregnant at the school, and that was enough for her. She promptly said, "Oh no, you're not staying in this school!" Quick like a bunny I found myself enrolled in North Miami Beach High School.

Did I say earlier that I never saw my father again after he left for "ice cream" when I was about three? Well, that's not 100 percent accurate. Just like the puff of smoke he disappeared in, he returned in the same mysterious fashion when I was around fifteen. I came home from high school one day and he was just there, assuming the role of head daddy in charge!

When he returned to our family for the second and final time, there were no explanations or apologies for his thirteen-year absence. No signs of brain damage or amnesia to potentially explain his absence. He just jumped right back into the driver's seat and took the reins of control. This man who knew nothing about me was there trying to tell me what I could and couldn't do.

Candidly, I admit that I never connected with my dad. If I had to describe this stranger in five words, I would use "distant," "cold," "stern," "bookworm," and "quiet." I remember the first night he came back, and we were having dinner, just me, him, and my mom, who was standing by the kitchen sink and I said, "Mom, can you grab me a fork, please?"

Before she could even get a chance to respond, he jumped in and said, "No, you go get the fork yourself!" Immediately, a wave of disgust ran through me. All I could think was who the heck does this guy think he is? I didn't understand why he was back in our lives and definitely didn't see the need for him. We had been doing just fine; my mom had figured it all out. He brought a negative type of energy to our home that had once been a happy one.

His presence definitely caused noticeable fault lines and cracks in the relationship between my mother and me. Nothing I could do was good enough or right in his eyes. If I would bring home a B on my report card, he would say, "It should have been an A." I remember my mother going out of her way to include him by inviting him to a play or dance recital and he would turn around and ask her, "Why do I need to go to that?" He never came. My father hardly smiled and created such an oppressive cloud over our house. If a boy dared to call me on the phone, he would be on the other line, trying to listen. I'd quickly hang up once I realized he was eavesdropping. Whenever I had friends come over to the house, they would pick up on his unwelcoming energy and it would mortify me. He actually earned the nickname Ayatollah from my friends and me because he was notoriously unfriendly and scary. My mother was suddenly no longer a factor because she conceded her power to him. She receded into the background in our household and became invisible.

Axel Jean-Pierre had missed out on so much of my life and never exhibited any regret or pangs of loss for doing so. He never saw my use or value and sadly gave me the impression that he never thought I would amount to anything. One day I would prove him wrong.

At some point, I stopped interacting with him completely and things became really frosty at home. This spilled over to my relationship with my mother, and I became disconnected from her as well. My new routine would be to come home from school and go straight into my room. I began to release frustration by creating drawings of tombstones with my name, birth date, and the current date drawn on the front. I was signaling that I was dying. So dramatic, I know; no wonder I became an actress! I prayed that they'd find the pictures and think I had died. I was hurting inside and felt like I was dying a slow death. Was it just the dramatic antics of a teenage girl, or was it a not so secret cry for help?

I would have nightmares that he was very mean to my mother and physically abusive to her, but I can't confirm if I actually saw anything in reality. Was it a waking nightmare? Have I suppressed some memories too difficult to face? I also remember consistently dreaming of a far-off doorway that I could never reach. I felt trapped. All I know is that when he lived with us, I developed very protective feelings for my mom. It was weird because this was a woman who had protected me my whole life. The roles had been reversed when he returned.

I recently saw an old picture of me with my dad when I was really young. My sister sent it to me because I had to use it for *The Real Housewives of Beverly Hills (RHOBH)*. I was laughing in the picture, but I don't remember many times like that between us. I felt no connection to that laughing little girl sitting on her dad's lap. I wish I knew what she was laughing at.

I don't understand what my mother saw in my dad to make her love him so much. I got the feeling that he was the love of her life out of all four of her husbands. Correction, three husbands. She married that bastard twice! Don't ask me why. To me there were no redeeming or endearing qualities. I couldn't grasp how my mother could be so strong, confident, and decisive before him and then flip the switch to crawl under his thumb. Haitian tradition is that the men rule the roost; or so they thought. My dad ruled everything. My mom always waited for him to get home before we could eat, and he would always get fed first. He didn't wash a dish or a cup in our house. He just looked on from his throne on high. And he was short too.

At some point, my dad brought his son, my supposed stepbrother, to live with us at the house. Not only did he miraculously reappear in my life, he also had the nerve to bring company too. I'm sure there was no thought of how it would make my mom feel. My stepbrother was about four or five years older than I was. Maybe this is the family he left to go and raise. Who knows? Our home seemed more crowded than ever, both physically and energywise, and my mom let it all happen without even discussing it with us first. I'm not saying she had to get our permission or anything—after all, it was her house and she paid the bills. I am saying she didn't give us the consideration of a heads-up to take the temperature of how it would make us feel.

It was really awkward for a young girl to have a guy living in her house who she didn't know. I was already in the young womanhood phase and feeling the awkwardness around that. On one occasion, he got inappropriate with me. He kept trying to get me to try things on him that crossed the line completely. He had said that he was my brother and wanted to "teach me stuff." I told my mom immediately, and that's when he got kicked out of the house, pretty quickly, after that. Too bad the old man didn't go with him.

Reflecting on the lessons I learned from my relationship with my mother, I recognize I was also taught from an early age that pleasing men and making them happy was the most important hallmark of being a "good woman," according to my Haitian mother. My mom catered to my dad, and before him to my brothers as well. She always put their needs above and before her own. In her eyes, this defined her as a very "good woman." I'm not debating her goodness as a woman, I only grapple with what she internalized as the source of her worthiness. Sadly, that's just how she was taught to exist in this world. Her worth was determined by their happiness and unfortunately stifled by the times in which she grew up. She was a good woman for so many other reasons, and it makes me so sad to know that I don't think she really realized it. Imagine what she could have done if she realized her true worth . . . her true power.

Then fate stepped in and changed my life forever! One day when I was sixteen, I was asked by a friend to be an extra in an orange juice commercial. I had no idea what an "extra" was, but I went with it anyway. At the end of the two-day shoot, I looked at the lead actress, a beautiful Black girl, and said, "I want to do what you're doing!" I went on to ask a bunch of questions as to how she got the job, but she was not giving up the goods, Biatch! I found some other people on the set and asked the same questions about how she got there and finally found out she was represented by an agent named Irene Marie of Irene Marie Models. To show you how green I was, I didn't even know what an agent was. I heard the name and looked her up.

Days later, without an appointment or even a headshot in hand, I was driving myself to Fort Lauderdale, Florida, to Irene's office to inquire about modeling. The balls on that girl! On my way there, I stopped at a traffic light, and there were a number of cars also stopped behind me. I leaned over to look in my side mirror to see if I needed to apply more lipstick. When I reached over to grab my lipstick out of my bag, I was completely startled by a hand reaching into my car with a business card. The voice attached to the hand told me, "You should be a model." The name on the card: Irene Marie. I later learned she was stopped at the same light, in a car behind me, and she saw my face in my side mirror. This was not just a simple twist of fate, this was God!

I worked quite a bit under Irene's agency and started building up my portfolio by doing test shoots. During that time, internationally prestigious modeling agent Eileen Ford, cofounder of Ford Models, would travel all over the country scouting for new young girls to sign to their agency. One of their stops was Irene Marie's agency in Fort Lauderdale, and I was introduced to Eileen Ford herself. I didn't realize how huge this was. She wanted to sign me on immediately. Part of her deal was that she needed me to move to New York City, center of the modeling world. I had made it into the big time. My mother was definitely apprehensive, but open to the idea. My father, on the other hand, flatly refused. To calm my mom's fears, it took Eileen Ford herself saying reassuringly, "All she needs is a toothbrush," and that made her feel better. Apparently, I was also going to temporarily move in with Eileen herself for a few months because the models' apartment was full. She liked me . . . she really liked me! She also believed that I had potential; who was I to second-guess Eileen Ford? I was hell bent on going to New York. Something inside of me said this was my shot. My tenacity was fueled equally by me wanting to escape from a tormented life at home and me running toward a career I had fallen in love with. I can't say what was the stronger pull for me. My mom was very cautious about and protective of us all, and I was her youngest child. She eventually pleaded my case to my dad and got him to begrudgingly agree with the move under one stipulation. He loudly declared that he had no intention of supporting me financially in any way. He threatened that I'd better find a way to make money and support myself, or return home. The "or return home" part was all I needed to hear to ensure that I would make my own success. Even if I had to sling wings at Hooters! To think, my journey started with a simple lipstick check in a side-view mirror and a set of brass balls!

I was so excited being on my own in New York City! I'm not going to lie; even though I was ambitious and gutsy, I was also terrified of this big, huge, bustling city and nervous of getting pushed in front of an oncoming train. I was wet behind the ears. Plus, while my parents allowed me to make the move, they had no intention of supporting me financially in this harebrained scheme to become a model. So what did I do? I hatched my own plan. Between modeling gigs, I got a fake ID and somehow found myself at the Playboy Club at Fifty-Ninth Street and Madison Avenue, where I officially landed a job as Bunny Garcelle.

It was an exciting opportunity that taught me more, and was way more complicated, than I expected. The world-renowned Playboy Club had a few different floors. All of them chic, sophisticated, and opulently decorated. There was a cabaret show on one, supper and bar on another level, and different private rooms spread out within the building. Every prospective bunny went through an intensive two-week training program to learn acceptable bunny protocol. We were taught the proper way to do the "bunny dip." It was a very precisely choreographed lean, or bend, that ensured you didn't reveal too much while serving drinks. We learned about endless garnishes for drinks and also had to know the drinks in the order they were set up in the bar area. When we would place our orders, we had to do it in the sequence the bar was arranged in. If your order was for an old-fashioned versus a whiskey sour, you had to know the right way to call it in to the bartender. It was definitely intense. I was always terrified they'd find out I was underage, so I worked extra hard to get it all right. We also had room managers that would mingle about and survey our interactions with the clientele. The place was a completely well-oiled machine. Then there was the bunny mother, who was the grande dame of bunnies. She was a beautifully elegant white woman with silky long hair that hung to the back of her thighs. Every night, before we could go onto the floor, we'd make a beeline for the locker room and start the meticulous process of getting dressed. First, we layered two pairs of stockings underneath a corseted bunny bodysuit. Next, we had bunny ears and a tail punctuated by button-on cuffs, which polished off the entire look. Before we could even think of going downstairs to the level where customers were, we had to go into the back office to see the bunny mother first. She would sit behind her desk casually dangling a long cigarette holder between her well-manicured fingertips. Between puffs from the skinny cigarette, she would look us up and down, squinting with a very critical eye. She would instruct us to turn around a few times so she could inspect if we looked "presentable" enough to enter the floor. If everything was in order, we were allowed to head straight down to start our shift. If anything was out of place, back to the dressing room we were sent to get it right. It was here that I fine-tuned my understanding of what it meant to present myself formally. This was my version of a summer job! I was determined to give my new life in New York my all. I knew that the risks I had taken paid off—and would continue to lead me to the life I desired. Fingers crossed.

Being solo in New York at seventeen, I didn't have any authority figures or role models around me to tell me what to do. I had to learn how to be my own everything in quick time. However, it's funny how you find guardian angels and father figures in different places. I remember I was dating this legendary R & B artist and producer named Kashif early in my career. He was so protective of me and would always have his driver, James, take me back to the city after I went to visit him. Fun-loving, popular, and edgy, Kashif was definitely a cool guy to be around and he treated me well. We genuinely enjoyed each other's company, appreciating our easy conversations both in person and over the phone. All was going smoothly until one fateful night while I was being driven back home. His chauffeur, whom I had established a pretty amicable relationship with, confided to me that he didn't think Kashif was for me. In fact, he said, "You're such a nice girl. I hate to see you doing this. Why would you subject yourself to this type of situation?" Knowing that James was usually a quiet man of few words, this statement was a mouthful.

"What am I doing? What type of situation are you talking about, James?" I replied. "What do you mean by subjecting myself?"

This was so unlike him, and it kind of ticked me off. He saw my disturbed glare and quickly remarked. "It's just that I think you deserve much better. You strike me as a really smart girl."

Now, this was entering very awkward territory for me. I kind of felt like he was crossing the line a bit. This man, whom I barely knew, was virtually questioning my intelligence, and it offended me. I always made really easy small talk with James as he drove me back and forth. I also found comfort with the older man because we were both of Caribbean descent. Whenever I would jump in the back of the car to go home, I would jokingly say, "Home, James!" So this new, stern and accusing tone was disturbing, to say the least. As it turns out, James wasn't trying to offend, he was trying to protect. Apparently, I wasn't the only fish on Kashif's hook. He was reeling them in left, right, and center! As James put it, "As you leave his house, he has another girl flying in right behind you." Great; I even had to compete with flying fish! Basically, I was on a carousel ride to nowhere and Kashif's bed was like an amusement park.

Looking back now, I can't tell you how much I appreciate that chauffeur named James. He risked his job and told me the truth even though he didn't know how I'd react. I respect that quality because I see it in myself. This honesty, I am sure, saved me possible heartache down the road and probably some unwanted venereal diseases as well. I never betrayed James's trust and I never repeated the conversation to Kashif. All I did, after getting home that evening, was go upstairs, sage my body from head to toe, and pray. Just like that, my sense of clarity returned and I never saw Kashif again.

The New York modeling world for a young, vulnerable teenager was a crash course in hard knocks and grit. It came with a boatload of rejection and required a whole lot of "suck it up buttercup" strength to get through. Even more, to be successful at it, especially as a Black woman in the 1980s. I had to learn to take care of myself out of sheer necessity. I was my only safety net, so I didn't have the luxury of failing. This is why, even today, I struggle big time with giving up control in relationships. I've had to rely on just myself for so long, it's a hard habit to break.

During that time in the modeling world, they were just starting to warm up to the idea of using Black models. Part of what I saw was that many of my Black contemporaries were giving into the pressure and having plastic surgery and nose jobs to make themselves look less ethnic. Shave a little here, lift a little there, and you were suddenly more "palatable" and marketable to a broader audience. A white audience. Even though I wanted this life so badly, I wasn't willing to do that. I loved my look and was proud of my ethnic features. I guess my mom's worrying about assimilation was unfounded; she had done a great job raising me to see myself as beautiful.

When I got my first *Essence* cover, after being scouted on a New York City bus by none other than acclaimed Black editor and journalist Susan L. Taylor, I remember frantically calling my mom to tell her. She was really excited and sent my dad out, a few months later, to buy copies of the magazine as soon as it came out. Wouldn't you know it, he ended up buying the issue from the month before, not even realizing that it wasn't his own daughter on the cover! Then, to make matters even worse, he would deliberately show off the incorrect issue to other people and tell them it was me . . . even though he knew it wasn't. I never forgot that deep level of hurt I felt. It's not that I expected him to call me up and act as happy and supportive as my mother had. That would have been way too much to ask. I just thought he might acknowledge that this was a great first step. Oh, and I also thought that he might recognize his own damn daughter. His own flesh and blood. It hadn't been that long since I had left.

My life in New York City as a teenage model was bananas! During the day, I'd be shooting all day with top photographers. One day in particular, I was told that I would be doing a shoot with Michael Jordan. The name didn't ring a bell for me, but I could tell, based on how my agent sounded, that I should be really, really excited. So I played along and pretended to be ecstatic. I'm embarrassed to say I didn't know who Michael Jordan was at the time. My kids might actually disown me if they read this. The next day working with him was so much fun. Everyone was running around catering to his every whim. For me, I was impressed by how tall and handsome he was. He took me on a golf date after the shoot and showed me how to hold a club properly and swing. It was definitely different and refreshing. He even invited me to join him in Hawaii. Like a naive little girl, I was "clutching my pearls" and shocked by the idea of going to Hawaii with a man I had just met. I graciously turned him down, and that was the end of that. Oh well, I blew that one!

At night, after working all day, I was being introduced to another game: the Studio 54 crowd. It was the place to be and be seen. Fabulous people, music, and paparazzi everywhere. It was like a beautiful glitzy circus. There I learned about Andy Warhol, how to really party, *Interview* magazine, and cocaine. Whose life was this? It was a loose, fast, and free time. One memorable night I recall seeing this striking-looking group of men and women huddled together tightly at a corner table with bright white powder on a tray. They briefly looked up, saw me, and motioned for me to come over and join them. When I squeezed myself into a seat around the table, one of the guys asked me if I wanted to have some of his cocaine. Not wanting to feel unsophisticated, I said sure with a casual air of confidence. As they handed me the tray, I awkwardly fumbled and spilled the entire thing all over the sticky table filled with half-finished drinks. Oops! Their jovial mood instantly flipped and the guy who offered me the cocaine immediately barked out, "Never mind!" and dismissively shooed me away. I decided this was the perfect "get out of jail free" card for me and I never touched the stuff again.

I was a seventeen-year-old girl making lots of money, and taking care of my mom and sometimes other family members financially. What I didn't realize was that making lots of money didn't mean you got to keep it all. Nobody told me about Uncle Sam. Paying taxes, or better yet, not paying my taxes, is a lesson I learned the hard way. I was never taught about finances, or the inner workings of what went into making money. As a result, I racked up a huge amount in back tax debt under a business manager who I should never have trusted. What does a seventeen-year-old know about taxes? Boy, have times changed. Today, my fourteen-year-old Jax has a greater grasp on financial literacy then I ever had well into my twenties. As a child, money was never discussed. Healthy financial choices and investments were not kitchen table conversations we had. Perhaps it was this way because money was always so tight, and my mom operated from a place of financial strain, worrying about making ends meet. She was on autopilot and flying by the seat of her pants. There were no trust funds, life insurance policies, or stocks and bonds waiting for me. No liquid assets or real estate holdings waiting to mature. With that as my financial reality, I worked hard to make money and worked equally hard to spend it.

From my early childhood, I learned how to turn lemons into lemonade. Instead of letting the fear of change, nagging insecurity, and rejection stagnate me, I used those circumstances as launching pads for my reinvention. My mother taught me this consciously and unconsciously. I soaked in all that I heard, watched all that I saw. Trying to figure out life and people's motives were hard. All I could do was use my limited knowledge the best way I knew how. Somehow I survived and thrived! I guess my *Sesame Street* lessons turned out to be the gift that kept on giving. I'm still a proverbial sponge to the world around me. I am a proud, observant, and obedient student of life.

Two

Motherhood

Raising the men I
wish I'd married.

—Garcelle Beauvais

I was married for the first time at age twenty-two and had my first son, Oliver, two years later. Decades later, I remarried and gave birth to my twin boys, Jax and Jaid, so being a mother and partner to men has long been my world. You can say I've got a PhD with the amount of firsthand expertise I've had with men and boys.

The reason I push myself to work extra hard, and guard my image so fiercely, is to be the very best role model to my three sons. To exemplify what a strong woman looks like for my newlywed son and my twins, who will eventually become husbands themselves. Their future wives deserve the very best version of themselves and so do they. I want to ensure that my boys all understand and appreciate the value of hard work, being open to change and the drive to persevere. The one constant I've had throughout my journey is that setbacks are a given. Trust me, my boys have had a front-row seat for many of them. They've also lived a pretty damn good life.

My kids have lived a life that has been far from typical. They've been exposed to a great deal of extravagances that include endless red-carpet premieres, cool swag bags, and meeting Hollywood icons most young kids only dream about. Outsiders see this access as a privilege and automatic blessing, which is mostly true. Despite this, I sometimes agonize about whether they appreciate their privilege. I'm not insinuating they're spoiled. I just worry that their criteria for what's "WOW" is overinflated. I am a woman who is proud of her success but hasn't completely bought into it. A woman who enjoys the finer things in life but hasn't accepted the embarrassment of riches associated with celebrity. Don't get me wrong, I know I work hard, but I also remember where I came from. That's my mother's voice constantly whispering in my ear.

My philosophy is that the struggles and plot twists are monumentally crucial to developing grit, character, and ultimately strength. Obstacles are transformative. If there is an absence of struggle, I question if there's anything of substance left in its place. More importantly, I'm nervous about what could be underdeveloped in these young Black men who will face a world of injustices stacked against them. Life is no red carpet for a Black man outside the bubble of Hollywood. I worry if my hustle and success will rob them of developing their own hustle and resilience. The irony is, I've worked so hard to give them everything I never had, but the gift of comfort could be the very thing that stifles their own journey. Hardship usually begets gratitude, and I want them to realize that humility is a powerful tool in life.

This is why I make the act of service and volunteering a huge component of my kids' upbringing. From an early age, it was important for my kids to give back. Simple things such as volunteering to clean up around their school on weekends and community service work were ingrained in them. On holidays, we would feed the homeless at the Los Angeles Mission. Every Christmas, we would buy toys, and also get toys donated, to take them to the Children's Hospital of Los Angeles. My boys would go down the hallways and give presents to the sick kids that were there. This would fill me with such pride and break my heart all at the same time. Even when they got too many gifts for their birthdays, we would put some aside to donate so they would understand that their abundance required them to give. To remind them of how lucky they were. To me, that's the balance that is necessary when you grow up in a world of such privilege.

My feelings are not without merit. "Regrets, I've had a few" as the song goes.

I had made a name for myself on top designer runways modeling for brands such as Calvin Klein, Isaac Mizrahi, and in print campaigns under the banner of the Ford Agency. I had already starred in *Coming to America* alongside Eddie Murphy. Not bad for an entrée into Hollywood and acting right? I was doing music videos, doing appearances on *Miami Vice* and *The Cosby Show*. I was making my mark in the acting world. I was still in my early twenties when I met my first husband, Danny Saunders, while I was doing a typical balancing act on the sidewalk juggling six shopping bags. He later joked that he should have seen this as a sign of my undying love of shopping. Danny was a strikingly handsome, smart, polished, and cool Jamaican man who carried himself with extreme pride and confidence. He was studying for the bar exam and worked at *Interview* magazine. He had a killer smile, a hot chocolate–colored complexion set off by gleaming white teeth, and a vibrant personality to match. He shared the same inner drive and zest for life that I had, and we clicked immediately. We were young, ambitious, and full of so many lofty dreams neatly tied up with white picket fences.

In 1990, when Danny and I found out I was pregnant with our first son, Oliver, I was nervous about being a mom and felt tremendous angst about bringing a new life into the world. I also had my career to think about. Being a pregnant model at that time was not something to be celebrated. It was actually career suicide, and that made me nervous as well. I needed some guidance in this new venture and couldn't wait to tell my mom the great news. When I told her I was pregnant, she was devastated! Her reaction really broke my heart. The way she saw it, my life was going to be completely ruined. She was tremendously hurt and we ended up not speaking throughout my entire pregnancy.

Here's a bit of trivia for you: even though pregnancy was frowned upon if you were an up-and-coming model at the time, Eileen Ford herself threw me a sweet little baby shower at her home. Another guardian angel of mine coming through in a pinch!

At the first sign of having contractions, Danny and I frantically called the doctor, who advised me to have a glass of wine and relax. Instead of calming my spirit, this advice freaked me out even more because I had been so regimented about cutting out drinking during my pregnancy, and now I didn't want anything to jeopardize this blessing. Instead, I took a shower and put on some makeup. After all, I wasn't planning on having this baby naturally! LOL. We were excited and ready to go! We jumped in the back of a yellow taxi and maneuvered through the streets of New York, feeling every single labor-inducing bump along the way. I felt like I was going to have him right there in the backseat! After arriving at Lenox Hill Hospital and being examined, the doctor informed us that Oliver would not be making his big debut for a while, so we had time to relax. Some of Danny's family, Shirley and Melvin, had arrived as well. Despite the doctor's predictions, someone never gave my baby that memo because within ninety minutes of checking in, Oliver was born with a headful of hair. He was screaming at the doctor and the rest of the world upon entry. We were ecstatic! We had done this together. Even though we didn't feel ready, having Oliver instantaneously felt right.

I called my sister Gladys right after giving birth and shared the happy news. She was so proud of me and delighted I had made it through okay. Then, like the wise "sister mom" she was, she told me to call my mom myself and share the good news. I figured that if she heard the news secondhand, that would only make our strained relationship worse. She would have felt slighted. I can't say I was thrilled with her advice, but I did as she suggested. When I got my mom on the phone, she appreciated the gesture as well. She said she loved me and only had my best interests at heart. It made me tear up when my mom confessed that she was afraid that I would abandon my dreams because I was about to be a young mother. She only wanted to see me soar.

Funny story: Being the young novice parents we were, after two days at home with baby Oliver, Danny and I were so startled by how light his skin was. Who am I fooling? We actually questioned whether they had given us the right baby. This baffled us so much that we called the hospital and said to the nurse, "Umm, excuse me, we are a Black couple that just gave birth the other day. We are all doing fine, but we just don't understand why our baby is so white."

I'll never forget how the nurse chuckled out loud and instructed, "Check his ears, dear. He will eventually become the color of the tops of his ears." Sure enough, within a few weeks, our little boy changed into a little chocolate drop right before our eyes!

What I remember most is that Oliver was a really happy baby. We were living in New York City and I was still modeling. I took Oliver everywhere with me. When I was working on jobs, I couldn't stand to be without him. I even hired a nanny so that she could help with Oliver when I brought him on the road. He was our everything. Within six months of giving birth, Danny and I packed up and moved out to Los Angeles because we didn't want to raise our son in a busy city center. For us, strollers, cabs, and subways didn't mix. I had also decided that it was time to fully commit to my transition from modeling to acting. Even after I had officially moved, my life was still very much a bicoastal one.

Jobs called and I went. Life was hectic and we hired an au pair from Sweden to ease the stress. During the Los Angeles riots in 1992, her parents got spooked and called her back home. They assumed she was "in danger," especially because they knew she was working and living in a Black household. After that setback, I scrambled and recruited Marie, my young niece from Boston, to help out. She had just graduated from high school and happily agreed to move out to Los Angeles. I had deep mommy guilt. Sometimes when I looked at Oliver's bond with Marie, it made me jealous. Grateful, but jealous. I will forever be indebted to her for making that life-changing sacrifice in the name of family. Marie provided the peace of mind I needed to be able to continue to chase my dreams.

I distinctly remember how independent he was even from a really young age. When I would take little Oliver to Mommy and Me classes, or preschool, he would happily crawl away without even looking back. Periodically, I would feel a pang of sadness, especially when I saw other babies clinging to their mother's skirt, crying for them to stay. Not my Oliver. I sometimes probed other moms to get their take on the situation, and they would say I was "lucky" he didn't scream and cry when I left. They would reassure me that this was a good sign that he was well adjusted and a free spirit.

Moving to the heart of the Hollywood scene was a big deal for my family. Suddenly, we were front and center rubbing shoulders with Hollywood titans. My role in Aaron Spelling's soap opera *Models Inc.* (1994–1995) led to my biggest career-defining acting role: costarring on *The Jamie Foxx Show* (1996–2001). My character was Fancy Monroe, and she lived up to her name in every way. This show became a big hit in the cultural vernacular of the 1990s and made me a household name (well, at least in some households). Even though I was technically "new" to the Hollywood hustle, it was an intoxicating whirlwind time. Everything was glossy, flossy, and flashy and I had a young baby boy who from the moment of birth grew up under a hyperintense version of "real life."

My marriage to Danny took a hit and officially ended. Now I was a single mom with a three-year-old son. Now what? The divorce was neither amicable nor easy. It was simply a relationship that had run its course and fizzled out. Danny wasn't as emotionally, financially, or physically supportive as I would have hoped, but that was indicative of the reasons why the divorce happened at all. He was a dreamer not rooted in the nuances of reality or the cost of it. I divulge this not to stir up any old ghosts of the past, but I can't explain where

I am without divulging where I've been. It caused me to have to over-compensate in all categories. I had to be more emotionally attuned, more financially driven; it was exhausting, and I was tired of chasing that dream. This is what led to my failed first marriage.

After the divorce, Danny would often say that I emasculated him. He felt I could afford to give Oliver more financial stability and material things than he could. The act of coparenting didn't go so well. To understand Danny fully, you also had to recognize that he had suffered a great deal of traumatic loss in his own life growing up. He didn't spend as much time with his young son as I would have liked because he felt like he didn't have "enough." He accused me of getting in his way of being a dad to Oliver. His apartment wasn't big enough. His job situation wasn't good enough. Danny was always driven by money, chasing that elusive big payday. He missed out on some really crucial times with his son waiting for everything to be "perfect," or right. Little did he know that his son just wanted his dad, imperfections and all.

My focus shifted to being there for my son and picking up the shattered pieces of our family. I did my best, but my life at the time was hectic and on the rise. Eventually, Danny and I came to a better understanding and he committed to trying to be more of a factor in Oliver's life. I had Oliver in the best school money could buy. The Center for Early Education was a place where you would plan your outfit the night before just to do a drop-off. He was going to school with Denzel Washington, Magic Johnson, and Bruce Springsteen's kids, to name a few. Whose life was this? Deep down, I feel like we squeezed into the school because they needed more diversity. By any means necessary, I say. I was a celebrity, with a lower-case "c," and I tried not to fan out every time I'd see Jack Nicholson pull in. To give you an idea of how affluent the school was, at a fund-raising event, they auctioned off the singular parking space they had for 20k . . . and there was a fierce bidding war for that bitch!

I was the little fish in a big pond. If I was in awe, I can only imagine what my young son was thinking when he would go over to twenty-thousand-square-foot mansions after school for play dates, or be driven in the back of a limousine to grab burgers. The principal of the school had to send home a letter to the parents pleading with them to stop trying to outdo each other with the birthday party theatrics. Some kids' parties had exotic animals, petting zoos, and imported snow. We were in LA, for God's sake! It was officially out of control. At the time I never fully grasped the totality of what fame, exposure, and too much access could do to a young and impressionable mind. I was busy trying to be a super single mom. Busy trying to be both breadwinner and trailblazer.

Oliver was adjusting to his new life and doing well in school. By the time he was in the fourth grade, school administrators told Danny and me that they thought we should test him for ADHD. They were seeing some inconsistencies in his learning and wanted to take a deeper look. Hearing the news, Danny was offended and adamantly opposed. He took the recommendation very personally and it hit him hard. Sadly, I deferred to him to keep the peace and went along with his wishes. We declined the tests and buried the warning signs. That's the sad thing about "maleness" in the Black community; sometimes it's inextricably tied to the illusion of perfection. Any hint of irregularities is a threat to manhood; suddenly you were considered broken. Today, with clarity and wisdom, I realize that I did my son a disservice. Not out of malice, but because I didn't trust my inner voice. At the time, my protective mother's intuition was screaming for me to listen to what the school was suggesting. I played myself small and silenced that voice.

Then, Mike Nilon, my second husband, came into my life. We were friends for a year before we started dating. My manager introduced us because Mike was an up-and-coming agent at CAA, the powerful and influential talent agency representing all the A-listers. Mike expressed an interest in meeting me because he was just starting out in the business. The only caveat my manager threw out was, "Don't ask her out because everyone does that!" He followed the rules and we had a cordial, platonic relationship at first. One day, however, we were in his car on the way to his friend's barbeque and he mustered up the nerve to lean over and kiss me. I was startled and confused, to say the least. I had never looked at Mike in that way, and this took me aback. Besides, I didn't want this to ruin the cool friendship we had built.

Mike was nice, smart, nurturing, and giving to both me and my son. He was a "safe choice," as they say. Not safe in the sense that I felt like I was settling. It was safe because I had made a conscious choice that I had no interest in dating a professional athlete, flashy rock star, or A-list celebrity. I wanted someone who was more grounded and would be there for Oliver and just be Dad to our future kids. He swept both Oliver and me off our feet. He was a great role model and nurturing spirit for my little boy. I was smitten too. On one of our first joint outings, together with Oliver, we took him to a theme park for the day. At one point, I went to the bathroom and left Oliver to wait with Mike. At that moment, Oliver chose to subject Mike to trial by fire by asking, "Where do babies come from?" Mike was freaked out, to say the least.

He hesitantly replied, "Ah, maybe you should ask your mother." When he finally told me about the incident, I laughed so hard. It was even funnier because I knew Mike had never really been around young children before. Just the fact that my son felt comfortable enough asking him that question warmed my heart and was the thumbs-up I needed. His answer was perfect, just like he was christened into the sometimes awkward world of being a parent.

Mike came along and what attracted me initially was that I felt like I had someone I could finally lean on emotionally, physically, and financially. Even though I was more than able to provide for myself and my son, it was nice to know that I had a reliable partner in my corner.

Looking back, I poured everything into that relationship to make it work. I liked the idea of Mike and me. On paper, we were a great match. He embraced Oliver like his own, and that alone sold it for me. Mike and I eventually married, and during this time of building my blended family, I admittedly began to overcompensate for having some of my attention redirected. I became too lenient, permissive, and selectively blind. Upon further examination, I noticed I would defer to Mike about what he thought was best for young Oliver. He based the input he gave on his own youth, but I knew my son. I remember times when Oliver was about twelve years old, he would ask to go out unsupervised with his friends, and something in my gut was telling me he wasn't ready for that level of freedom. There was that loud inner voice again; it was alerting me to something. I knew my son, but I would give in and defer to Mike because of course he knew best. Also, he was a man, and I was raising a young one. I thought for sure he knew best. Oliver was approaching his teenage years, and that alone would bring its own set of troubles. Unfortunately, his challenges weren't "regular" teenage problems.

This is the section of my story where I struggle the most with sharing above all others. I have wrestled for months with it. I knew at some point I would write a book about my life; but I didn't know it would be so hard. I am at a point where I am feeling freer and more fearless than ever before in my evolution. What trumps everything that I feel, or inner progress I've made, is my fiercely protective instinct toward my kids. I've tussled and I continue to do so with sharing every single ugly detail of Oliver's years of unrest. What I will confirm is that it was ugly, messy, and full of heart-stopping incidents that no family should have to go through.

Oliver was exposed to the best of everything and the most of everything. Pair that with too little supervision and you have a powder keg waiting to explode. I always took comfort knowing that I raised a compassionate, kind, and respectful young man, but what

I did not give enough credence to was that he was also extremely sensitive and emotionally vulnerable. He had a void that I couldn't see. How that chasm got there I am not completely sure. I can speculate that maybe it was because Danny and I broke up. Perhaps it was because he might have felt left behind and displaced once Mike came into the picture. Was it biological, or did he have a chemical imbalance? These are all speculations of a parent trying to grapple with how best to heal her broken son. Today, after years of therapy, tears, and heartache, I can painfully admit to myself that I took my eyes off the ball with Oliver. I assumed that because he had the best of everything, everything would work out for the best. Unfortunately, that was not to be the case.

Angst, fear, helplessness, and worry were consuming emotional daggers that governed my relationship with Oliver's teenage and early adult years. I was constantly on edge and always standing on high alert to extinguish the next catastrophe or problem. I forgot what restful sleep meant. I would cry myself to sleep at night and wake up in a haze of worry the next morning, only to start the cycle all over again. I had agonizing physical reactions to all the turmoil as well. You see, I suffer from severe eczema, and my body would break out in extremely painful rashes and it would be debilitating. The outside world never saw this pain. I am an actress, after all. This training came in very handy. It allowed me to compartmentalize my own reality and get into the mental space to perform at my job and provide for my family. I'm genuinely an upbeat person, but I've also had decades of playing different characters, projecting different realities. I leaned heavily on my resilience and relied enormously on my deep faith in God's mercy and grace. Throughout the contentious years with Oliver, my mother would remind me, "A parent's biggest struggle is that they are always as sad as their saddest child." I spent decades being deeply, privately sad.

My family did everything to try to help Oliver. I relied heavily on Marie to try to get through to him because they had that bond. My sister Gladys, in Florida, offered to have him move in with her family, but it wasn't the solution either. There were endless prayer vigils and gut-wrenching battles, but nothing worked. Mike's family, in small-town Milford, Pennsylvania, graciously invited Oliver to come live with them for a year. Hesitantly, I thought a simpler, more rustic life away from all the excesses would serve him well. I was extremely grateful for Stephanie and Joe Decker, but that didn't work for too long either. Toward the middle of his stay in Milford, Oliver was out of control again and we were at our wits' end. I put everything on pause and rented a house in the backwoods of Milford just to be close by to make sure he finished his ninth-grade year. To top it all off, I was in the middle of trying to conceive via in vitro fertilization with Mike and under great stress of my own.

I am a notorious scaredy-cat. Afraid of the dark. Afraid of critters. Afraid of scary movies. . . . As I mentioned before, I was going for a "rustic" experience for Oliver. I clearly didn't process the word "rustic" fully, or visualize exactly what it meant. During my time in Milford, I rented this really old house (or barn thing, depending on your perspective) in the middle of nowhere. I mean nothing but dense woods, bushes, hungry wild bears, chirping frogs, and crickets nearby. The first night Oliver and I got to the house, it was pitch black darkness everywhere. You couldn't even see your hand in front of your face. I decided that I wanted to try to lighten the mood; it had been a difficult reunion for us. I decided that we were going to light a fire and warm the place up a bit. We go over to the fireplace to kindle the logs already there and both jerked back like someone had physically shoved us! We were hollering like banshees. Laying right there in the fireplace was a dead bat! A vampire bat, if you ask me. My mind started to race as we cowered together in the corner. *I'm-NOT-cut-out-for-this-SHIT!* I thought. I have to admit, I couldn't help it, but I thought this was like a hilarious *Green Acres* city mouse meets country mouse moment. Oh well, we found a way to make the best of our remaining time there. The things a mother does for love, I tell ya! There was so much out of control and even more I couldn't control.

Upon moving back to Los Angeles, his troubles escalated quickly and we were at our breaking point. This is when we decided to have an intervention. Our first of many.

Even though Oliver is my son, and we lived through the turmoil together, I do not feel the intimate details of his struggles with addiction is my story to divulge fully. I say this not because I wish to hide, or feel shame for the hard times. Every family has struggles with addiction in some form or another. It took me a while to get to that place mentally and embrace this realization. Where I sit today, I learned how to stop torturing myself for not being able to recognize and save my baby from his pain. Part of the reason I found peace is because Oliver doesn't hold me, or his father, responsible for his choices. Again, God is great!

Today my Oliver is making positive strides toward progress. He is a new husband and a new father. He is all in. It gives me such pride to see him being the man I knew he could be. An amazing, thoughtful dad to my beautiful grandson Oliver Jr., OJ for short . . . that acronym took a little time for me to cosign on. I love the relationship he has with his new wife, Sam. In some ways, she saved his life, gave him purpose, and healed his spirit. She gave him something bigger than himself to live for. He is creating new music again, positively channeling his energy, his angst. He is so damn talented; he always has been. He carries himself with a new air of hopefulness and forward-looking levity that are contagious.

Oliver today represents the best of me. He is kind, nurturing, caring, creative, and madly complicated. Just like his mother. Do I have regrets? Don't we all as parents because we had the audacity to embark upon this crazy journey of trying to piece together and shape the life of another human being? Regrets are the guardrails of my life. My regrets raising my first son helped me be a better mother to my younger boys, Jax and Jaid. A few years ago, when they were about eleven, I agonized about how to share Oliver's struggles with substance abuse. I was afraid to expose them to the raw truth behind my pain because, in some ways, I didn't want to give them the idea that drugs were a pathway to problem solving. I cherished their innocence. I was nervous that they would see their big brother in a flawed light. In reality, the beautiful irony is that because of his struggles and inner fortitude to fight back from them, Oliver has become an even bigger source of inspiration for us all. My heart swells and tears flow being able to share that. He opened my eyes to the beauty in unvarnished truth. The truth that God uses the least of us to bring out the best in us. I have my son back! Not perfect, but back. We are healing as a family and in a good place.

The reason why I end this portion of my story here is out of a deep, abiding respect for the man Oliver is fighting to become after an almost two-decade private roller-coaster ride through hell. My gut tells me that just because I am able to share my pain of dealing with a family torn apart by the ravages of drug addiction doesn't mean he is ready to have his private truth consumed by others. I honor and respect that. I have learned that shame is only felt when you haven't unpacked heavy baggage you carry. When you haven't admitted that you are human and allowed to falter. He is not ashamed of his past, just trying to make peace with it the best way he knows how. Soberly, quietly, peacefully. One day at a time.

Living a life in a fishbowl is a difficult and oftentimes love-hate relationship. You fight and claw to get noticed on the front end and retract and contort to stay anonymous on the back end. One of my greatest joys is that I think I have raised sons who know how to think independently and are not afraid to give voice to their thoughts. Mostly it makes me burst with pride and hope for the future, and other times it drives me absolutely crazy.

A few months ago, I was filming a scene for my second season of *The Real Housewives of Beverly Hills* and I had my boys at home with me for the week. It had been an unusually difficult week during the middle of the COVID-19 lockdown. Everything I was working on now had to be brought in-house, and I was working from home. Tucked away upstairs in their rooms, the boys were navigating on-line schooling as well. I had also started filming for *The Real* in my guest room, which became my makeshift studio. It was organized chaos, but chaos nonetheless. After a day of wrapping up filming *The Real* portion of my day, the *Housewives* crew rolled in to capture my home life while I packed to go away on a trip. Well, normally Jaid is amicable and easygoing, but on this particular day he was just over it all. Over me, over my glam team, over the camera crew, over it all! He flipped a switch on me like never before and refused to play along and engage. It was cringeworthy for me because I was genuinely torn as a mom, but I also was acutely aware that it was my job he was boycotting. This was a package deal. I was mortified, embarrassed, and pissed as hell at his outright disrespect and, quite frankly, his rudeness. I had never seen this side of him before. He had turned into one of those damn Gremlins they tell you never to feed after midnight!

After everyone had packed up and gone home, and we had re-treated to our neutral corners, Tazz, my longtime family friend and assistant, pulled me aside and gave me a dose of truth and reality. She said, "Girl, you know he really wasn't having it today to act like that. Jaid is usually more patient," she stated. "You have to allow him to vent even when you don't feel the same. He was hungry and just wanted to eat something. He didn't want a camera in his face. There have been crowds of people coming in and out of his home nonstop for the past week. He was done and he had enough! He was crying out for his peace and space but didn't have the words to articulate his frustration. So, like any kid would, he showed out!" she added for good measure.

I sat there silently and took in what she said.

This voyeuristic life is hard on me and equally hard on them. I realized I had to give them the space to voice their frustrations and vocalize their feelings. I was just afraid that once the footage of the scene was out in the world it would get misinterpreted as him being a typical Hollywood brat; which couldn't be further from the truth. At least they were a bit older, more mature, and could process things a little better. One of the perks I had considered when I agreed to do the show was that I could be at home more for my kids. I had been traveling for work a ridiculous amount and they were getting a bit older. I felt that this was the time I needed to be a little closer to home for them so I could remain engaged.

Later that day, my other friend Nicole and her husband, Chris, came over and I shared the story of Jaid's outburst and heard the same justified response from them. Nicole reminded me that reality isn't always pretty or neat. She pointed out that I shouldn't be afraid to show the fact that my kids were normal, sometimes cantankerous, preteen boys who found their mother annoying from time to time.

Lightbulb moment; sounded just about right! Leave it to kids to keep you grounded. You can be adored by millions, but at home you are just Mom. This is my reality.

The only exception was the nugget of "male wisdom" that Nicole's husband, Chris, offered up when he joked, "Just wait. He's going to thank you for the spotlight later on when he realizes how many girls it's going to allow him to rake in." And just like that, I had to laugh. It takes a village, I say!

Even in my own little nuclear family, I see how different men's personalities and temperaments can be. The unexpected and random laughs you get through parenthood make the tough times melt away (well, those and a little Prosecco, of course). My very independent, cerebral son Jax called me late one Sunday night as I was prepping for my hectic week ahead, reading scripts and preparing comments, and the conversation went like this.

"Hello, Mom, it's Jax. I wanted to ask you something."

"Okay, Jax," I replied. "Is everything okay?"

"Ya, everything is fine. Do you remember the time when you tried to get us to do some modeling with that agent and we said no?"

"Yes, I do. Why are you asking?"

"Well, I've reconsidered and I think I would like to try and do some modeling," he went on to confidently inform me.

"Okay," I said, holding back a giggle. "Can I ask why you've decided to give it a try now?" And here's why I love my brutally honest little boy.

He said, "Well, yes. Of course, a big part of it is because I'd like to make a lot of money. And second, I thought I'd give it a try while I still can!" Upon hearing that last line I almost fell off my chair laughing. I didn't see that curveball coming. Damn it, man! At age thirteen, my son was not only hatching a plan to stack his bank account, probably so he could get his own apartment. He was also contemplating the biological clock running out on his fictitious modeling career! Kids say the funniest things, I tell you. This definitely made my night.

All of my entanglements with men and young men reminded me of a really deep conversation I once had with some friends who also had young sons. Our conversation revolved around our battle wounds, "First World" war stories, and uplifting tales about dating and loving in today's world. When I reflect on that conversation, I realize that at the heart of those laugh-worthy, cry-worthy, and cringeworthy tales was how we as women loved our men.

As an island girl, I recounted, as did my friends, that there's an ingrained cultural way of thinking that led us to see men, and our relationships with them, in a special light. In the old days, our mothers were conditioned to serve and worship their men—even more than themselves. They were taught to expect very little but give to the point of exhaustion. This is what a "good woman" was supposed to do. Times have changed, and so have women. We are more self-assured; exercising our freedom to excel in many ways, and maneuver alongside our male counterparts.

We reflected on our mothers who had superhigh expectations of us as their daughters. Demanding we "act right" and never dare offend, or act offensively. We spoke about the less forceful stance they took with our brothers. Somehow the boys in the family were always allowed to be less than participatory, less than responsible for their actions, and less than accountable for their inactions. It dawned on me that this is where it all started, built on a platform of unequal expectations.

Because my own father was more a figment of my imagination as opposed to a fixture in my life, I created my own version of what I thought a father should be. Both young men and young women need their father equally. I would be lying if I said I didn't miss the idea of having mine. Each child needs varying doses of life skills from their dad, for different reasons.

A common phrase that women usually use is that "men have to change." In my own life, I have come to really question this statement. I believe that there is another side to this statement, which puts some of the onus back on us as women. I would say that we as women have to change. Change how we love our sons. In doing this, we will help them eventually become the men that women want to love in the future. I am paying it forward. I believe we should hold them responsible when needed and allow them to cry and feel deeply when necessary. We can't nurture the toughness in them without acknowledging and encouraging their compassionate and loving side as well. To have a complete man, both must coexist in equal increments.

Let that sink in for a minute.

We have to be careful not to coddle, ignore, and permit behaviors that release young boys from taking, and accepting, responsibility for their actions. We have to remind them to be careful, kind, respectful, and thoughtful in their speech and actions, equally. After all, words have power. We must teach our sons that strength comes in many forms.

We are our sons' first female relationship. We owe it to our young boys to give them the necessary burden of responsibility from a young age. It can be as simple as chores around the house, or service in the community. Every moment is a teachable one.

Speaking of teachable moments, the "Me Too" movement had me on high alert. When this movement took flight, I promptly called a family meeting and discussed the concept of consent with my boys. To make this confusing issue easy, I gave them the simple analogy that it was akin to the act of choosing a movie that we all would see. "Before you go see, we must all agree!" I told them.

Our awareness has changed so much and has to be embraced on every level. Admittedly, I never had these conversations with Oliver. Moms, dads, grandparents, and caregivers; every voice of influence must be on the same page. I can't say my son Jax was listening. He swiftly gave me the "talk to the hand" gesture in objection and adamantly informed me that he was not ready for that type of conversation. Mentally, I giggled and gave him high marks for his honesty. He was self-assured and forthright enough to tell me he had heard enough. That's my Jax! Clearly, I was barking up the wrong tree with that one. He wasn't ready. Jaid, on the other hand, sat up straighter and pulled in a little closer ready to hear more. His entire body language changed when he heard the word "sex." I've got to watch that kid. I swear those two couldn't be any more different for twins. I always joke that they just hitched a ride together to get here but went their own separate ways once they slid out of the birth canal.

As an immigrant mother with two interracial sons, celebrating diversity is so important to me. The proud Haitian in me wants to make sure my boys are confident in their cultural roots. It's why I published the *I Am* trilogy of children's books. When I would take them to the library, I couldn't find any books that celebrated diversity, where they could see themselves in the characters, so I published one. It helped me start a conversation with my boys where I could start to explain what people might ask them and how they might respond. I wanted to proactively make sure they had the words and tools before they, or the kids around them, started asking a lot of questions about race. I have never forced them to choose whether they identified as white or Black. In some ways, they identify as both. If you ask them, they proudly describe themselves as young Black men . . . their choice.

When I was looking for someone to write the foreword for the *I Am* books, I approached my friend Halle Berry (name drop) and gave her the manuscript. She read it and immediately called me and said, "I wish there was a book like this when I was growing up. I always had the feeling like I had to choose between one parent or the other. I felt like I couldn't fully embrace both sides." That's what I wanted to avoid for my boys . . . they deserved more. So did other kids like them.

Even before the uprising of the Black Lives Matter movement I had "the talk" with Oliver as a young man. I was looking at a young brown-skinned man running around in an affluent, predominantly white neighborhood, and it scared the heck out of me. Yes, I had the conversation about keeping your hands at ten and two on the steering wheel while being stopped by a police officer. The yes sir, no sir responses necessary. I ingrained in him that he shouldn't make any sudden moves in the midst of an exchange with a cop. It broke my heart to do it, but it was a matter of life and death if I didn't. So now, when the rest of the world finally woke up and realized that these conversations were happening in Black families as a necessary rite of passage, I had to ask . . . Where the hell have you been? As a Black woman, I don't know what it's like to live in a world of selective awareness or such relaxed denial.

My reality on race and my interracial twins was summed up in a conversation I had with Mike during the height of all of the George Floyd protests. For reference, Mike is one of the most racially aware non-Black men I know. Being a Philly boy, he grew up very entrenched in Black culture and fell fully in love with it. Mike even played Division 1 basketball in college. Even with this knowledge and exposure, Mike confessed to me that he was scared for our boys. He soberly analyzed the fact that when our boys go out in a group with their friends, depending on if the friends were Black or white, this would determine how they were seen and, sadly, treated by society. With their white friends they would be seen as the "Black kids" and with their Black friends they would be seen as the "white kids." This terrified him, and he didn't scare easily. No matter how "good," educated, or "well mannered" we raised our sons to be, society would still see them as Black first.

This is how the wheels of change begin to churn. Slowly but surely. One family, one conversation at a time. It breaks my heart, but also fills me with hope for a safer, more tolerant, and inclusive future. The truth is, everyone has a stake in the cost of achieving racial equality; some just haven't embraced it yet.

My personal approach to parenthood, as you can see, is about fluid conversations about any topic whenever the opportunity strikes. I vowed that my kids will be seen and heard! We, their fathers and I together, are empowering our kids to build a better future. This is my most important legacy and my love letter to my boys.

Three

Marriage and Love

Single doesn't always
mean lonely. Relationship
doesn't always mean
happy.

—Anonymous

Honestly, I don't know how I feel about actually saying "I do" again. However, if I did jump the broom, I know exactly how I would do it. "Picture This, My Dream Wedding!" Of course, it's a destination soiree on a Caribbean island!! Kissed by the morning sun, I slowly open my eyes, waking up to find myself in a beautiful, oversized four-poster bed. Loosely anchoring each post are sheer muslin drapes creating a mystical canopy above. I roll over to soak further in the goodness of the crisp white sheets that smell like lavender drizzled in honey. As I slowly emerge from my fog, I realize where I am, sequestered in a gorgeous bungalow oasis steps away from where I will begin my new life with the man I love. Fifteen-foot ceilings accented by heavy rustic beams and antique mango wood doors add a warm earth-toned glow, making the room feel so quaint and elegant. Pale, sand-colored walls mixed with neutral-toned decorative rugs and pillow accents create a clean and inviting space rich with texture and opulence. I am in heaven!

I hear a knock at my room door. It must be room service delivering the breakfast I ordered the evening before. As I free my legs from under the layers of billowy covers and step onto the cool Italian marble floor, I have a big smile that won't subside no matter how hard I try. I'm trembling inside with excitement and heady anticipation for the day ahead. I let in the gentleman from room service and lead him through the whitewashed French doors leading out to the terrace, where he methodically begins to set up a charming breakfast table for one. From across the room, I notice the gleaming, polished silver cloche server, no doubt concealing a yummy assortment of breakfast fare. *Now, this is class*, I think.

After room service leaves, I slowly make my way over to the table where the smell of fragrant coffee is calling my name. Passing by a floor-length mirror along the way, I get a glimpse of my reflection; I feel beautiful! In the center of the breakfast table, I notice a magnificent arrangement of pink peonies, gardenias, and white hydrangeas with a small hand-written note carefully tucked inside. I reach for the note and my eyes mist over as I read the words "I can't wait to make you my wife." Swoon! I clutch the note to my chest, and tears begin to flow. . . . I am finally at my perfect wedding day! A day I never thought would come again. My future husband (TBD) has surprised me with the perfect destination and an elegant gathering of all the people I love, here to share in my joy. I sit on the terrace, slowly sipping my coffee as I enjoy nibbling on croissants with fresh berries, all while soaking in the breathtaking ocean views. I am thanking God for my blessings and his promises fulfilled.

About an hour later, my glam team and bridesmaids arrive. My gorgeous, fitted mermaid gown with lace overlay train is displayed on the door to my dressing room. My heart skips a beat as I fall in love all over again with the sparkly crystal embellishments on my dress. Someone pops a bottle of Cristal champagne; 1990s R & B music begins to play, and my room suddenly transforms into a festive pre-show to the big event.

After sliding into my gown and doing final touches on my makeup, I step out and greet my three sons to start the ceremony. My bouquet of choice for my fantasy wedding day? The hands of my boys, which I will hold as they walk me down the aisle. You see, I feel that brides spend so much time picking out that perfect dress, then end up hiding it behind a bouquet of flowers just as all eyes are on them. Nope, no bouquet for me, thanks!

When we make our way to the outdoor aisle, I am greeted by seats filled with fifty to sixty of my closest family and friends. My three boys are at my side, sharing in my joy. As I make my way down the aisle, I can see my future husband's face beaming with pride. I have no reservations, and my heart fills with love. I take one final sigh of contented relief. All the pieces of the puzzle have finally fallen into place. All the hurt from my past has melted away. I have found the man of my dreams! My forever love.

I am truly a hopeless romantic at heart; the Hallmark Channel ain't got nothing on me. This is how I see it: Marriage is not the pinnacle, or end goal, to my romantic life. If it happens, it happens. I want a man but I don't *need* a man. There's a big damn difference. I've spent some deep soul-searching moments readjusting my thinking and refocusing my energies toward the type of qualities I want in a partner. If it comes with a ring along the way, it does. If it doesn't, I will have a beautiful life with a person I am thrilled to be with.

I'm past the point of looking for someone who is going to make my life happy. I've worked really hard to accept the reality that I'm responsible for that. That's too heavy a burden to place on somebody else's shoulders. Happiness must first come from within. It's meant to be shared and enhanced, not generated—especially if it's authentic joy. What a partner hopefully will do for me is provide support, companionship, external love, and nurturing. It's no longer hard for me to admit that I would like a man in my life. As I said, I want a man but I don't need one! I've grown into this and I'm continually evolving. That's me, finally learning to embrace my pink side . . . my vulnerability.

The strange thing is that, growing up, I saw my mother and grandmother as such strong, independent women who never let absentee men ruin their lives. They survived countless setbacks and rejections but nonetheless accomplished great things. My mother, in particular, absolutely never gave up on finding love. The only sad part about this is that she equated her value as a woman with how that love was received by the men she chose. She didn't put a value on the intensity and selflessness of the love she gave. Rather, she internalized the cruelty of the lack of love she received back. She never required very much from her male loves to make her happy. Cheat and lie and you will always have a home here. That's what she taught my dad. After all, as women we teach men how to treat us. Both by our actions and, even more importantly, by our inactions. Most of us just haven't come to this realization yet.

Growing up in my household, I never saw what lasting, nurturing male/female relationships looked like. My mother was married and divorced three times. My grandmother's husband ended up leaving her with three kids to care for on her own. From my youth it's safe to say that my frame of reference regarding strong, devoted, and loving male figures sucked.

My first marriage, to Danny, found me at a time when I was trying to find myself. We had only known each other for two months before we got married. I was clearly in a rebellious phase. We were both much too young, definitely inexperienced, and still fumbling our way through the adult world. I was attracted to Danny for all the right reasons but stayed long past the warning signs reared their ugly heads. I believed in his dreams and ambitions wholeheartedly because I knew he had the smarts and personality to make them happen. I was a dreamer myself after all and was only in New York City because I acted on my dreams. He was so smooth and charming, qualities that meant a great deal to me. I could easily see him integrating into my world. I think his charisma struck such a chord with me at the time because most of the island men I had encountered, at that point, were a little rough around the edges. He was different. He always knew what to say at the right time and to the right person. He gave off a confidence and polished sophistication that drew me in; perhaps this was because I was also working on perfecting those qualities within myself. Regardless of the whys, I was hooked. And we were married within two months of meeting each other.

After multiple professional rejections, I began to notice a change in the man I had fallen in love with. Once we had our son, Oliver, Danny was under a great deal of additional pressure trying to financially carry his growing family. Remember, he had that Caribbean machismo running through his veins. He was so proud of becoming a dad and wanted to live up to the ideal of what that meant. On the surface, this was admirable and exactly what I hoped for. Unfortunately, as a result of the stress and ego, we began to see the world differently in deeply fundamental ways. I was optimistic, he was pessimistic. I sought out solutions to obstacles, he looked for scapegoats to blame.

I searched inward, he blamed me for all that was wrong. It became too heavy and too oppressive. We argued constantly, and I could no longer feel the joy and love that first attracted me to him. Remember, we had only known each other two months before getting hitched. He, or perhaps we, had become different people.

The bigger I was becoming in my career, the smaller he seemed to want me to shrink. Perhaps it wasn't conscious, or intentional, but a result of his own hurt and unresolved issues with his troubled past. Either way, it became too much and too costly. I distinctly remember being really close with Angela Bassett in my early days in Hollywood. She was kind, fun-loving, and a very generous spirit. She would always call and invite us to parties and gatherings with her. In essence this went against the grain of everything you hear about backstabbing, competitive women in "the business." We were both Black actresses, fighting for the same spotlight in a city that had room for only one at a time if you looked like us. Whenever she would call, I was thrilled and wanted to go, but Danny would always find excuses for why we shouldn't. To please him and ultimately keep the peace, I would decline the invitations. Angela eventually stopped asking and we drifted apart.

We were just so very different, or maybe never really had anything in common after all. The relationship became claustrophobic and the problems too insurmountable to fix. I decided to end our marriage of almost nine years. Oliver was three years old.

I became a single mom. I was a little older, wiser, and more cautious. I was laser focused and enjoying a great acting career costarring on *The Jamie Foxx Show*. Without having to wrestle with a failing marriage, I gained clarity and drew on my inner strength, which allowed me to continue to heal, parent, and work on my craft.

With Mike, my second husband, I thought I had solved all of the issues from my previous marriage, because I had selected someone so different; and not because he was white. He was the polar opposite in so many ways and provided the security I was looking for as a single mom. I came as a package deal, and it was no longer just about me. After we had dated for two and a half years, we came to a cross-road because I felt it was time for us to move the needle forward. I had that same conversation that most of us have with their man at some point . . . the "shit or get off the pot" talk. He said that marriage wasn't part of his "five-year plan." Mike had become a top agent at Creative Artists Agency (CAA), one of the biggest talent agencies in Hollywood, and was focused on his rise to the top. He chose to get off the pot, and I had to let him go.

We didn't have any contact for a period of time. Oliver and I both were sad and felt a void with his absence. About three months later, I went to a movie premiere with a friend and bumped into him unexpectedly. And out of the blue right there at the premiere, he asked me to marry him. In 2001, we officially sealed the deal, and then rode off into the sunset and lived happily ever after, right? INSERT sound of record scratching HERE!

No marriage is ever easy, no matter what outward appearances may suggest. Mike and I were making it work. Dealing with Oliver's mounting problems, simultaneously trying to conceive children of our own, and juggling two red-hot careers on the rise. We were "that couple" to be envied, and we lived an enviable life by all outward appearances. The powerful agent marries the actress sort of thing. Romantic vacations in Italy; we did it all. Invitations to the Oscars, going to *Vanity Fair* parties, you know, all the typical Hollywood couple stuff. We had bought a big house and would throw these huge Christmas parties that Gwyneth Paltrow, Ben Affleck, and all types of influential Hollywood people would attend. We became a big staple in Hollywood.

I was almost forty, and the road to conceiving a child again was not an easy one. There were multiple unsuccessful rounds of in vitro fertilization treatments and many heartbreaking setbacks full of self-doubt and questioning of God's plan. Despite three miscarriages (that number three again), life-threatening fibroid surgery, and hectic work schedules, somehow God's plan was manifested when we finally found out in 2007 that we were pregnant with twins! God is good all the time and all the time God is good.

Once our boys arrived, Mike continued to be reliable and attentive. All the things that made me fall in love with him. I knew I could count on him, which gave me the peace of mind to feel comfortable and safe. Because we had twins, there was no room for traditional mother/father rolls in our household. We each had our own kid, plus Oliver. He was an all-in dad and completely hands on. Jax was a crier but Mike showed an amazing amount of patience and tenderness toward him. It was beautiful. He would willingly change diapers, make bottles, do nighttime feeding all without being asked. He often woke up before me on the weekends and gathered the boys, strapping one to his chest in a BabyBjorn and the other in a stroller. Fully prepared, he'd set out for early morning walks in the neighborhood. He cherished his daddy time. One particular morning I remember him telling me that two older ladies had stopped him and marveled at how much men had changed regarding their level of parental involvement. They praised him and said it was so nice to see him taking care of the boys himself. He loved every minute of being a super dad. Yep, that was Mike. Perfect on the outside.

Have you ever had the wind knocked out of you and the rug pulled from beneath your feet at the same time? I have. It happened like this.

Almost nine years into our marriage, Hurricane Betrayal hit the Beauvais-Nilon residence. I was shooting a pilot in Atlanta, and Easter weekend was coming. Holidays are always an extra-special family-focused time for me. I was scheduled to be in Atlanta over that weekend because I was still filming. I begged the producers to wrap my scenes early and let me go home Thursday night so I could spend Easter weekend with my family. I also knew Mike's parents, Jack and Rita, or Pop Pop and Gigi, as the kids call them, were coming into town from Philadelphia for a visit. I love spending holidays with family and I adored his parents, so this was important to me. I was thrilled when the producers agreed to release me early. I immediately called Mike and told him the good news and asked him to pick me up from the airport. His reply was, "Why don't you take a car?"

This response surprised me. I even passed the remark "Well, if we were courting you would have picked me up!" After a bit of back and forth he finally agreed.

I remember getting to the Los Angeles airport and having to wait outside on the curb because Mike was late, which is one of my biggest pet peeves. My philosophy is, if I can travel from somewhere far, you should be able to pick me up on time. Logical, right? When he finally showed up, he came around the corner to grab my luggage. As he was rounding the corner, a strange feeling welled up in my soul, and out of nowhere I heard myself faintly muttering the words "That's not my man." I don't know why, but that feeling overtook me unexpectedly.

My hair was really big and curly at the time, and he said something about it that sounded very disconnected and remote. Something offhanded like, "Oh, fuzzy hair!" There was just something very artificial and forced about the way he said it. I get in the car, we're holding hands, and I'm saying to myself, *Garcelle, stop whatever you're thinking. He's a good man. He's a good father. Stop what you're thinking!*

We finally get home that night and by this time Mike's parents and the kids are all asleep. I go into the boys' room to stare longingly at them sleeping peacefully. I give them kisses and go to bed myself. The next morning, we wake up, make love, and I decided I was going to make banana bread because everybody in the house loved my banana bread. I get the boys and go downstairs; our nanny, Indira, arrives, and Jack and Rita come downstairs as well.

Indira then reminded me that the boys' preschool was having an open house that day and I said, "Oh good, we should all go. That way Gigi and Pop Pop get to see where the boys go to school. It will be fun!"

About an hour later, Mike, myself, and the boys set out for the school in our car, and his parents follow us in their rental car. Everyone was in high spirits and ready for a fun day ahead. We get to the school; we're having a great time and the boys are so proud to show off their school to their grandparents. Rita announces that they were going to head to the market so they could grab something to cook for dinner later that evening. About five minutes after they leave, we were preparing to leave the school as well and I say, "Oh shoot! I should have asked them to pick up something for me." Since I had been traveling so much for work, I knew I didn't have it at home. Before strapping the boys into their car seats, I began rummaging around in my bag for my cell phone and realized that I had left it at home in the rush to get out the door. Realizing this, I casually turned to Mike and asked him if I could use his phone to call his mother before she left the store. Little did I know that this would be the beginning of the end of our happy little family as we had known it.

As Mike was giving me the phone, I reached back to catch one of the boys who was about to take a tumble. With that awkward motion my finger must have accidentally pressed the button for text messages, and it pulled up his last text. When I looked down at the phone, I saw three simple words, "I love you," in an unread message. At first I thought I had sent it. Then I did a double take and realized I didn't recognize the number at all.

I immediately felt an uneasy feeling grip my body, and my

adrenaline began to race. I forcefully blinked a few times rereading the words just to make sure they were real. "I love you"—yep, that's what it really said right there in black and white.

I turned to Mike, holding up the phone so he could see it, and said firmly, "What's this?" He glanced at the phone and his face immediately changed and his body stiffened. Busted!

He immediately shot back, "It's nothing! It's nobody! It's nobody!" He had a panicked look of guilt all over his face. He went stark white and I could see him mentally searching for another answer to give me. Any answer other than the truth.

I responded, "Who is it, Mike? Tell me who!"

I guess I must have asked the question a few too many times because I could hear my son Jax chiming in from the backseat pleading with his dad, in his little person voice, "Daddy, tell her who! Daddy, tell Mommy who!"

I still hear Jax's little voice today echoing what I asked during those moments of revelation. With that interruption from the backseat, we stopped talking and fell into a deep silence for the rest of the ride home. Everything I had believed, security I had felt, and truths I wholeheartedly internalized all went up in flames in seconds. I could feel the pain and the pressure welling up behind my eyes, and the dam was about to break. All I could think of were my poor, sweet boys, and this pushed me over the edge. The tears that I had desperately been holding back began to fall.

We get back to the house and Pop Pop and Gigi had already made it home. I said to Rita, "Will you watch the boys for us?"

She looks at me skeptically and says, "You look like you've been crying."

"I think Mike is having an affair," I blurt out. Just like that, no beating around the bush.

She holds me by my shoulders looks me dead in the eyes and says, "No, no, no, he doesn't have it in him!"

I go upstairs and see Mike pacing back and forth in the bathroom. I plead with him over and over again to tell me the truth.

"I'm sorry," he says as he sits down hesitantly on the edge of the tub.

Through tearful sobs I demand, "I need to hear it directly in your own words! What are you sorry for?"

"I've been having an affair," he lets out. I pushed him to tell me for exactly how long. "For five years with someone in Chicago," he finally confessed.

The room started spinning. I didn't know what to do, or how to do anything past that moment. Everything became foggy, unclear, and definitely engulfed in rage. I suddenly found myself lost and disoriented in the familiar comfort of my own home. I was stunned by his admission that the affair had been going on for five fucking years! Even one month would have been too much, but five freaking years? It was too unbearable to comprehend. As my mind started to race backward to search for missed clues, all of the whys, hows, and logistics of the infidelity that I wanted to know started to clutter my mind and stumble over each other to come out of my mouth. All I could do was sit there silently for a minute sobbing to myself uncontrollably.

I finally yelled back, "You know your parents are here for the weekend, right? I'm not going to pretend. You need to go downstairs and tell them the truth. I refuse to fucking pretend!"

"I'm not ready to tell them yet," he stated flatly, catching me a little off guard.

"Well, you better beat me to the bottom of the stairs, then," I spat back vehemently and with firm conviction.

I abruptly left the bathroom and quickly headed downstairs. The boys were sitting in their high chairs chatting back and forth and eating their snack. Mike entered the kitchen right behind me. He knew enough about me to know that I wasn't playing. Rita and Jack were both already there, cooking.

As we entered the room, everyone stopped what they were doing and looked in our direction. Mike starts out by announcing to his parents, "I have something to tell you. I've been having an affair." I pushed him further and told him to disclose how long it had been going on. He spoke, "For five years."

Upon hearing the confession, Rita took a deep sigh of breath and collapsed into a chair by the kitchen counter. Jack lowered his head, opened the backdoor, and slowly walked outside into the backyard by himself.

I was confused and utterly disoriented. I went upstairs and called my best friend, my niece Marie, and told her what happened. She immediately offered to come get me and the boys and step in as my steadying force. I ached to hear my mother's soothing voice of wisdom, but I had lost her two and a half years earlier. I felt so alone and especially hurt because I knew how much my mom had loved Mike as well. KeKe would have been so deeply hurt and disappointed. I didn't sleep a wink that Friday night because I was sobbing uncontrollably, with deep hurt and betrayal ripping at my heart. At some point in the wee hours of Saturday morning, I picked up my phone and wrote the infamous email titled "What do Tiger Woods, Jesse James, and Mike Nilon have in common?"

I had to go back to work in Atlanta the next day whether I liked it or not. You can only imagine what a restless weekend I had. On Sunday afternoon, I was in my closet mad as hell packing my suitcases and sobbing. Mike came in; I was sitting on the floor and he was standing up. I can't remember exactly what he was saying, but there was something he said that made me feel like, *Oh shit, it's not just that one girl in Chicago.*

The "email heard around the world" was initially sent to a small group of our close, trusted friends at CAA, where Mike worked. I didn't hold anything back and revealed how blindsided I was by his infidelity and how it had impacted our family. I hated him and wanted our friends to hear directly from me exactly what he had done. I just knew they would be as shocked as I was. After all, this was not my shame to bear. Unfortunately, one of the "trusted friends" with whom I shared my raw, honest pain leaked it publicly and exposed the messy situation to the world. I had been betrayed again. I was mortified!

By the time I got back to Atlanta, the producers had already heard what happened. I was in the makeup chair crying endlessly, and the makeup artist was trying to stop me from crying while applying my makeup.

One of the producers came into the trailer and asked, "Will you be able to work today?"

I quietly said, "Yeah." And I worked. I'm not quite sure how I did it.

Over the next four or five days, I finished shooting the pilot and then went home. I had kicked Mike out of the house during that time, but he had to stay there with the boys until I returned from work. I told our nanny that I wanted to take the boys to the zoo to try to make it fun and keep it as normal as possible for them. My nanny and I arrive at the zoo, unbuckle the car seats, wrestle with the fucking strollers, get to the first animal, and my phone rings. It was my publicist, and she said, "Garcelle, I have something to tell you. *Us Weekly* is coming out with a story that claims there's been multiple women. Multiple affairs."

I felt sick and fell to my knees. Luckily, there were no paparazzi following me that day or else they would have gotten that shot. I am an instant wreck! I turn to Indira and tell her we have to leave immediately. The boys were understandably upset and screaming, "Why are you leaving? Why don't we get to see the animals? Why are we leaving, Mommy?"

As we got back to the car and Indira is strapping Jax and Jaid back into their car seats, I call Mike from outside of the car and I say, "This is the call I just got." I give him a brief rundown and say, "What do you have to say?"

He said, "I'm not going to answer that until we're in front of a therapist."

I looked at my phone in disbelief and screamed, "Fuck you! You just answered it!" Click. I hung up. There was nothing else to talk about.

Looking back now, I realize just how unremarkable the infidelity in my marriage was, especially based on Hollywood standards of marriage. Nonetheless, it was remarkable to me. I can't say that for days and months after the incident I didn't wrestle with the notion of working things out and taking Mike back. We even did couples' therapy and had grueling back-and-forth exchanges. We had two little boys, after all. We also had history, a public image, and had built a nice life together. And, let's be honest, no woman wants to start all over again in her forties. Despite these urges, I also had the very real perspective of what a lack of trust and undeserved forgiveness can do to a woman's soul. A big reason why I never tried to work it out with Mike was because this, or rather these affairs, were not isolated incidents. This was just who he was. I realized that if I stayed in a relationship with him, it would have changed the very essence of who I was as a woman. I would have become that insecure wife gripped with anxiety and doubt every time her husband left the house. I would constantly be sneaking into his emails, looking at his texts, questioning his phone conversations. I wasn't willing to go there. More importantly, I wasn't willing to have my boys grow up with a mother so preoccupied and consumed by such insecurity and mental anguish. I saw my mom go through it and I didn't want to be her. Not like this. Not this time.

As the legendary musical genius and civil rights activist Nina

Simone once said, "You've got to learn to leave the table when love's no longer being served."

I filed for divorce from Mike in May 2010. Jax and Jaid were three years old when the divorce was finalized. There it is again. That number three keeps lurking in the background of my life and popping up in unexpected ways. I had three boys, my father left my mom when I was three, I left Danny when Oliver was three, and now this. I don't believe in coincidences. Remember? I can't fully understand yet why the number haunts me like it does. I guess this means my work here is not yet done.

My knee-jerk reaction to change was always to equate it with defeat. My second divorce hit me even harder than I had expected because it was on display for the whole world to see. By my midforties, I had grown accustomed to having the titles "wife" and "mother" attached to my name. I thought I had mastered the art of being a "good woman." I was in a great place in my career and optimistic about what the future held. I hated the prospect of having to start over from ground zero and open up myself, in a romantic way, all over again to someone brand-new. Especially as a single mother with three kids. It's only more recently that I have been able to readjust my thinking and embrace the idea that starting over doesn't necessarily mean going backward. I am constantly reminded that sometimes God chooses things for you that he/she knows you don't have the strength to choose for yourself. Letting go and letting God, as they say.

I still love being in love, always have, and always will. I still believe in finding "the one" . . . my one. By nature, I'm an eternal optimist, a glass half full not half empty kind of gal. In spite of my less than ideal relationship models and two very tough divorces of my own, at heart I remain hopeful about finding my happily ever after. It must be the hopeful Haitian in me. Not in a childish fairy tale sort of way built on the fantasy of someone sweeping in to "rescue" me from single life. Nothing dramatic like that at all. Besides, I've been rescuing myself for the past four decades and have done quite well. I am not looking for someone to complete me, either; I'm learning how to fill in all of the gaps myself and appreciate the negative spaces. Actually, I hope I never reach completion because that means I've stopped learning and growing on this journey called life. I'm just leaving myself open to receive that special one who can and will have my back, like I would have theirs. Oh, and some great sex too! Hey, a girl still has her needs.

Learning to lean into my own vulnerability allowed me to tackle the idea of dating again. After Mike, I didn't have sex for a very, very long time. Did I emphasize long? I had to make peace with my needs, wants, and desires and not interpret them as a lack in my own womanhood. I don't always want to be so strong by myself and for myself. Despite my disappointments and past failures, I still love the idea of having a partner in life and a shoulder to cry on. An intimate, physically soothing shoulder that gives me a release, both physically and emotionally, from reality. I appreciate my family, children, and village of girlfriends immensely, but not even they can fill that void.

The challenge with being a single woman living alone for so long is that you get used to never having anyone to lean on. I had built a solid life for myself through my own blood, sweat, and tears. Literally. Men like to know they are needed by a woman. That's how most men are taught to define their masculinity. The damsel in distress concept didn't only claim women as its victims, it also engulfed men as well. When women embraced their independence culturally, it also messed up traditional male roles. Now, because women don't necessarily need men to be the sole breadwinners, it has shaken up relationship dynamics. Personally, in my most recent attempts at relationships, I have found it hard to put away my superwoman cape, let my guard down, and embrace my softer bunny ears. I did that before and it didn't work out so well. Remember? I've had to learn that even the most secure man still wants to have a woman who is soft, delicate, and not always jockeying for control. This is not a bad thing, it's a natural thing.

It's the constant fight that we independent women of today have. We've made so many monumental strides, huge leaps and bounds, but in making this progress, I feel we must resist the urge to trade in our femininity for a pair of newly found balls. I am still a woman and fully embrace all of the wonderfully embedded nurturing qualities that make me female. Mother Nature herself is both beautiful and powerful. These are equal but opposite strengths, and they exist in us.

As a side note, another discovery I've made is that I have learned to love sleeping like a starfish in my bed. Just me spread out fully on my back like I'm making snow angels. I don't have to compete for any blankets or fight for the remote before bedtime. This is my happy place and one of the perks I've found to being single.

I've come to realize that it's more important for me to learn what I don't want in a partner than to focus on what I do want. In my own case, I have way too many firsthand experiences encountering qualities that can torpedo a relationship into an abyss. These are the qualities that made it onto my deal breakers list, my own personal no-fly zone. I've learned no more financial projects or men under construction. No more controlling guys who have issues with successful independent women. No more emotionally void or unavailable men. I like baggage, but only with a Louis Vuitton or a Chanel logo on it. No liars, no small thinkers, and no insecure dudes either. Oh, and no dudes with skinny jeans. Above all, I require honesty and respect, even if it hurts.

There are two types of change: willing and forced. I have come to see that both have their blessings. Perfection in a mate is not my goal. I constantly affirm that it's not about finding a perfect mate, it's about finding a mate perfect for me. Someone who is with me because they think I'm perfect is not the one for me either. If perfection is your perception of me, I will surely disappoint you because I am far from perfect. I recently dated someone who couldn't stop reminding me daily of all of my shortcomings and missteps—let's just say that didn't last too long . . . plot twist!

For me, disagreements are a necessary evil. They can be toxic or constructive, depending on how you handle them. If I'm going to be with you, we need to be able to disagree fairly and respectfully. It's a huge part of learning to interact authentically with another person. Because I'm such a strong personality, or have "dude" tendencies, as I've been told, I need someone who's strong enough to give me a mental push back when I've gone too far. This is all part of the honesty I seek. A friend always reminds me that she would never marry a man she hasn't had an argument with. Her philosophy is that she needs to see how someone is going to lock horns with her, so she can determine their true character. You learn a lot about someone in the throes of an argument. When their guard is down and emotions take over. Mike and I never had a fight, and now I understand why this always drove me so crazy.

My voyage toward finding my proverbial G-spot is 95 percent metaphor and 5 percent practical—if I had to quantify the process. What I mean is, I have learned through time, mistakes, and much experience that my perfect mate can't be summarized by any one particular category. Nor can my "perfect man" be reduced to whether he gets a passing grade in the bedroom. I tend to grade on a curve anyway! I'm much more complex than that, as I think most women are. I'm not difficult, but complex, which is an important difference. They carry different intentions behind them. In my eyes, being complex is more about being flexible and seeking the right fit. Difficult is about being bitter and mean-spirited; that's definitely not me. I am complex in my wants but not difficult or unrealistic in my expectations. I am not rigid in my beliefs in traditional male/female roles. I do, however, still hold a dash of traditional norms at heart. I prefer a good, old-fashioned phone conversation over a text any day. I like to hear a man's voice and hear the meaning behind the words he's saying. I like a man who thinks to hold a door open for me. I'm not helpless by any means, but I do like the idea of having a man around to help. Even when I can do it for myself, as I am learning to let go. My love language is in sync with acts of service. Acts of service received and also reciprocated.

Speaking of giving and receiving, it's never too late to be more sexual, and it's never too late to teach an old dog new tricks! Discovering my comfort level with sex was not an easy or an intuitive journey for me. Growing up in a very strict Haitian household, sex was never spoken about. To give you an idea how taboo the topic of sexuality and sexual development was, my mother never mentioned anything to me about menstruation. I mean not a peep. I distinctly remember when I was ten years old and got my first period. I sat frozen and terrified in the bathroom for hours, fearing I had been shot and was bleeding to death. My first instinct was to run to my older sister Carole for answers. There were no cute milestone marking "coming of age" celebrations like you see today. I was left to figure it out on my own. True story.

One of the only sex "conversations" I can recollect my mom having with my older sisters was that she let them know she had some specially brewed tea for them to drink the morning after they went out on a date. She tried her best to hold tight and was really strict on us dating in general. What was the special tea? Why was it so special? Well, it was her version of the morning-after pill, aka plan B! Made from exotic Haitian herbs and roots all boiled and steeped together. This Caribbean concoction was supposed to prevent any surprise pregnancies from happening. KeKe wasn't going to let anything stand in the way of her daughter's chances for success and advancement. She was taking things into her own hands.

Imagine her shock and horror when soon after coming to Miami to live with us, from being with her father in Montreal, my older sister Chantal announced she was pregnant! The news was like a roach bomb that went off in our house, because it impacted us all. The horror, shock, and shame my mom felt. She was mortified. Not only was her teenage daughter pregnant, she also got pregnant on her watch! So much for the "special tea"! Even though she had seven children, to this day I wonder if my mother ever felt fulfilled sexually as a woman. Or was having a bunch of children just another indicator of being a good woman? Hmm, another topic for my next therapy appointment.

Predivorce, and even during my marriages, you would have thought Missionary was my middle name. It's not that Haitians are not sexual people, Haitian women were just taught to be reserved and quiet about our sexuality. Deep bases in Christianity and purity are at the core of this reserve. Certain topics regarding your body were taboo and unspeakable. Even though as Haitians we are generally loud and outspoken, we clam up really quickly on matters of being sexual beings. I couldn't get my reserved upbringing out of my own head. I played sexy roles on film, but in real life, I wasn't huge on experimentation, or "coloring outside the lines," as Carrie Bradshaw put it. Besides that, I never really talked openly with my female friends about their bedroom antics. It's so ironic that now on my podcast, *Going to Bed with Garcelle*, that's all I do; it's surprisingly therapeutic.

One thing I did love, and that I feel gave me a leg up on the competition, is to give blow jobs like it was my second job. I liked the act of taking hold of a man's penis, admiring it, teasing it, and vocalizing my approval during intimacy. Active role playing—or setting the table, as I call it—is my jam. Let's just say I know how to pump up a man's ego during the act of oral pleasure, which makes him happy to report for duty. This gives me a sense of power, and I love the control aspect of it. Lord, I hope my kids never read this book!

Now that I was newly single, I had plenty of downtime and a vagina that twitched constantly. I was also preparing my backup arsenal and picked up two fresh new vibrators waiting to get worn the hell out. One was dark chocolate and the other was white chocolate. You never know what flavor a girl's going to want, so like a good soldier, I wanted to be prepared for anything. Oh, and I purchased a twelve pack of C batteries so there'd be no awkward interruptions during "game time." There's nothing worse than hitting the right spot and then having your vibrator go on strike before you got what you came for, so to speak. My goal was to figure out my sweet spot, and right now I was focusing on my labia. All of my years of having sex, I struggled to find what made this woman happy and sexually satisfied in bed. I had never been taught that a woman was entitled to her sexual pleasure as well. Now I was fully in charge and on a relentless mission. Just the act of openly admitting I used vibrators was a huge boss move for me. It gave me the ability to control the outcome and tempo like I had never done before. I was always assured my happy ending.

It was a slow process for me reintegrating into actually dating again; well, at least a live person. I already had a running date, Monday through Saturday, with Ebony and Ivory (that's what I nicknamed my battery-operated friends), but even I couldn't fool myself into thinking that self-pleasure was the last stop on the train for me. I was still young, vibrant, and in love with love. I am a hopeless romantic! Outwardly, I had shaken off the sting of my second divorce, come to a great place with my ex where we were coparenting beautifully, and learned to forgive and leave the past in the past. It took a lot of work, therapy, and retweaking of my inner narrative. I was at a crossroads in life because I was now in my fifties and comfortably making a new normal for myself, by myself. The only areas I hadn't fully begun to work on were dating, my sexuality, and my emotional fulfillment as a woman.

Enter Darnell, an average-height, chocolate-skinned brother who was far from average everywhere else. His silky voice was like a hot knife through butter. His teeth were all perfectly aligned and blindingly white against his rich complexion. Sporting a chiseled, athletic frame flanked by nicely toned arms, he loved to wear Slim Fit shirts just to make sure you saw how fit he was. I remember he would give a sexy chuckle right before he would call my name, using his seductive voice. Damn, I swear I almost had to run and put on a new pair of underwear every time I would see him sauntering in my direction. As you may have guessed, this was a man who I had tremendous sexual chemistry with and in the words of the great congresswoman Maxine Waters, I was now ready to reclaim my time!

Confident, sexually liberated, and jaw-droppingly more adventurous in the bedroom, I was sweating bullets trying to figure out how to keep up with this dude. To top it all off, I was nursing a bad back and fighting off a bout of eczema that was raging all over my body. I was a hot damn mess, but like a true champ, I couldn't let him see me sweat. I bought some killer new lingerie, sexy fur-trimmed bedroom heels, and flavored lube, slipped into acting mode, and went to work, honey! I was reinvesting in me and getting one heck of a return on my investment.

Even though Darnell was more sexually advanced than I was, he was the type of man who made me feel comfortable, safe, and free to explore my fantasies. Through his patience and understanding, he gave me the freedom to shed my layers of fear and insecurity about being a good girl and how it didn't have to mean being prudish in the bedroom. The acrobatic tricks I was pulling off made me forget I was even a mother. In the bed, in the kitchen, on the stairs, and even on top of the washing machine, I was getting my back blown out! Finally, I felt confident in exploring and questioning the norms of what I had been raised to believe was acceptable behavior. You can say I was finally discovering my G-spot like I had never done before. All a girl needed now was a good chiropractor.

The funny thing about coming into your own is that it radiates from within. Even my girlfriends noticed the change. I remember that one of them remarked, "Ooh girl, something's different!" It was in the way I walked, talked, and carried myself with a different glow. That morning-after glow.

This sexual gladiator was a big exhibitionist. This is one area I never considered myself a prude in because I've never been offended by healthy episodes of PDA. If the mood strikes me, I love to hug, kiss, and be openly affectionate with my partner in public, and I'm not put off by others who do similarly. With Darnell, it was a little beyond that. He was turned on by the thrill of potentially getting caught in the act. Listen, I'm a mother of three and have built a solid public reputation that I had to consider. Getting caught doing the "walk of shame" is one thing, but I couldn't risk doing a potential perp walk! This portion of the program made me uneasy within my soul. It nagged at me constantly and caused me to shrink away from him instead of rise to the challenge. I couldn't even enjoy the sexual thrill of it all because I was too busy keeping lookout!

What I found is that there's a fine line between wanting to perform sexually for your partner and feeling like there's a spotlight on and you HAVE to perform. There we were, him dressing up in just a sexy bow tie and cuffs and me dressing up like a sexy nurse on Mondays and Thursdays. The lotions, potions, endless toys, location scouting, and death-defying feats; dating this man was exhausting! Mentally and physically, it was an exercise in trying to outdo myself. I felt like I had to up the production value every time I saw him. This was Survivor: Sexcapades Edition!

Whatever happened to just enjoying the person you're with

without all the excessive bells and whistles? Was our attention span that short? Was this ADHD sex? In my opinion, a bag of tricks is only special if you don't whip it out at every gathering. Otherwise, it just becomes a worn-out bag of clichés. How long could a relationship fueled by constant performance art last? I began to question if he wanted me physically, or if he was more interested in the production of it all.

What happened to Darnell? Well, that Lamborghini was way too much maintenance after a while. It finally dawned on me that I needed a simpler, yet reliable, Mercedes-Benz that could withstand the millage of life. But I have to admit, it was really fun taking that Lambo for a test drive a few times around the track!

As if dating and finding meaningful connections weren't hard enough, then the coronavirus shook the world. I can't lie; I seriously began to doubt if I would ever have sex again. My single girlfriends and I would sit around on FaceTime and half-jokingly scheme up scenarios for how we could orchestrate COVID-19-compliant dates. Never mind a sex life with anybody new. That alone would surely require an NBA type of bubble situation. During this time, I resorted to working with a dating coach. I was leaving myself open to new experiences. I was fixed up with this really nice guy who seemed to have everything I was looking for . . . on paper. He was tall, very financially successful, nice, caring, and attentive. He liked to talk on the phone, was age appropriate . . . things started out really well. Our first conversation lasted thirty-five minutes. The second, ninety minutes. This escalated to a few really enjoyable FaceTime calls. He was easygoing and nice to talk to. Wow, this was off to a great start. I even changed my MO (modus operandi) and never shared the budding romance with my girlfriends for fear of jinxing it. I was trying to change my pattern of behavior in hopes of getting a more favorable result.

A few more conversations in, he half-jokingly started to drop hints that he thought most women wanted "sugar daddies." He didn't seem too cool with the notion of taking care of a woman financially. He later went on to invite me to watch a world-famous virtual magic show. Apparently, it was a really hot ticket. He said he planned on watching it with his girls and said it would be nice if I joined in and watched with my boys. He even told me that he had just purchased his tickets. Instead of making the gesture to purchase the tickets for me, he sent me a link to where I could buy them for myself. Now, call me crazy, but something about that turned me off. Not looking for a sugar daddy myself, this shouldn't have bothered me at all. Why it struck such a chord with me was that his approach screamed of someone who was not overly generous and not very giving. I am a giving and overly generous person and need someone who takes no issue with reciprocating. Needless to say, that fizzled and burned really quickly, but I applauded myself for not ignoring the signs and honoring my own no-fly zone.

Romance is a big deal in my book. I don't necessarily subscribe to the concept that you should meet each other halfway. Here's why. Someone who has only 50 percent as their ultimate goal in a relationship is not the one for me. I want someone who is willing to go all the way. All out while wooing me—yes, I said wooing. All the way with having my back. All the way with giving me truth even when I don't want to hear it. I want the type of love, admiration, and respect for someone that compels me to give freely because I know it will be reciprocated. By my calculations, if both parties have 100 percent as their goal, then no one should ever feel they're getting the short end of the stick. Nobody likes a short stick.

A guy who takes care of himself and pays attention to the finer details of his appearance is a big turn-on for me. I want someone polished because I pride myself on working hard to always "present" with pride. This is an ingrained practice my mother always taught and modeled for me. "Always look your best even when you're feeling your worst," she would say. KeKe, my mother, would put on lipstick to go to the mailbox, honey. Living in the spotlight has taught me to stay ready for anything at all times, and your physical appearance is a big part of that. A man who I find attractive understands and lives that concept as a personal choice. He doesn't always have to be suited and booted, but just aware that his physical presentation speaks volumes about him even before he has a chance to utter his name. This is a lesson I constantly drill home to my boys.

Only God knows where my romantic life will lead, but as sure as I'm Black, I know I will be ready to greet it 100 percent of the way. Until then, I give myself permission to enjoy doing the field research and making mistakes along the way.

Four

Infertility: Perfecting Resilience

Sometimes we're
tested. Not to show
our weaknesses, but to
discover our strengths.

—Anonymous

This chapter deserves its own space because the issue of infertility sneaks in plaguing and devastating the lives of so many unsuspecting women in every age bracket, race, and socioeconomic background. This is my story.

Hollywood is where I work, not who I am! I have no problem taking off my lashes at the end of the day, slipping on some jeans, putting my hair in a scrunchie, and getting down and scrubbing scuff marks off my kitchen floor. I know about digging deep and giving any task your all.

Resilience has been a recurring theme throughout my life. Having it in your work life is one thing; the financial compensation and rewards usually motivate you to keep pushing forward. Mastering it when faced with life's challenges and hardships where control is not an option is another story. My grueling bout with infertility in my second marriage taught me that. It was a long, rocky road toward having my two beautiful twin boys, a five-year-long ordeal, to be exact. Everything I thought my body was created to do, and had done easily before, backfired. Because pregnancy happened so easily for me the first time around, I had no idea how the female body worked or how miraculously unpredictable conception and carrying a child to full term really were. Everything affected your chances of pregnancy. Stress, your age, chromosomes, when you first got your period, and how close you were to menopause; the list went on and on. I was happy and settled in my marriage and really wanted to fill in the family unit by having a child, or children, with Mike. We did everything they said you should do to get pregnant naturally. Then, on two separate occasions, when I did manage to conceive, I had miscarriages. When we realized that what we were doing wasn't working, we sought help from a fertility doctor and started the process of treatment. At the start of the process, the doctors noticed that I had fibroids and instructed me to have them removed. Doing this would greatly increase my chances of conceiving and keeping a pregnancy, they said. So I did as the doctor advised and had the surgery.

Soon after, I had a catastrophic setback. I was working on a television show called *Eyes* for ABC at the time. One day, I started getting these excruciating stomach cramps and did not know what was happening. I powered through, finished the scene, and went home after I was done shooting for the day. When I finally got home, I noticed the pain had slightly subsided. Two days later, the pain came back with a vengeance, and I thought I was dying. Mike was out of town so I called Marie to take me to the hospital. In the emergency room, they couldn't figure out what was causing my pain. Before I was about to be discharged, one of the doctors ordered an MRI for me. When I finally made it home, I laid my head down on the pillow and my phone rang. Marie answered it, and all I remember is that she said the hospital had called and said, "Bring her back immediately, we have to perform emergency surgery on her right away!" Turns out, I had developed a life-threatening bowel obstruction from the fibroids surgery and my waste was backing up in my system and poisoning my body. If I hadn't gone to the hospital when I did, I wouldn't be alive today to tell my story.

After that ordeal, I was shell-shocked and terrified. I broke down and confessed to Mike that I felt like we shouldn't pursue the IVF route anymore. I thought my body was telling me that it couldn't handle it. It was a bad omen for me out the gate, and I was spooked. With that notion firmly planted in my mind, we decided we were going to give foster care a try and adopt a child. After all, there were so many children already out there that needed a home. Like dutiful and eager foster parents to be, we went to foster parent education class on Saturdays for two weeks. I quickly realized that this option also had its hardships and pitfalls. After the first class, I cried all the way home. I was devastated over the thought, and potential reality, of falling in love with a child who wasn't guaranteed to be mine. If we decided to commit to this process, we faced the very real possibility that eighteen months later, the child's biological mother, or parents, had the legal right to take the child back if they could prove they were fit parents. It was too much for me to bear. I was already so raw and exhausted from going through so many setbacks and physical disappointments. I couldn't stand willingly opening my heart up to that level of heartache. I felt hopeless and broken. I would cry and pray night after night. I was completely down on my body and felt betrayed. Nobody had ever explained these types of womanhood struggles to me. In my family, in my experience, if you wanted kids, you just had them. My mom had seven of her own with no problems. My sisters each had multiples of their own. What was wrong with me?

Even though IVF was an expensive and invasive process, with zero guarantees, we decided to revisit the process and give it another try. I'm pretty sure no woman's first choice is to do IVF, but we found a great doctor named Dr. Ringler, and he gave us hope where there was none. We implanted one egg at first and got pregnant right away. Six weeks later, I had to have a D & C (dilation and curettage, or abortion in laymen's terms) because the baby stopped breathing. I was devastated once again! A D & C is the last thing you want to do when you're having infertility problems and desperately trying to get pregnant. I was heartbroken no matter how normal everyone told me it was; I felt my body had failed me yet again. We decided to try one last time. It was all I had left in me.

Rigid monitoring of my hormone levels, follicle counts, checking monthly calendars, self-administered needles in my stomach, and patches galore; Mike and I were on a wild roller-coaster ride with no seat belts. It was mentally and physically exhausting. I remember dragging myself into the doctor's office every other day for monitoring. I would overhear other women being informed about their follicle count, which is the indicator of readiness and optimal conditions for implanting embryos. Numbers in the range of eight to ten were constantly being mentioned, which was fantastic—for them, at least. It definitely added to my anxiety because I knew I was working with a significantly smaller count—far from the point of being ready. I subconsciously developed a deep follicle envy, which added to my emotional tug-of-war.

I also had this toxic inner guilt that I wasn't able to give my new husband biological children of his own. He was such a great stepfather to Oliver. I would always replay the same thoughts and questions in my head. Maybe if Mike would have married someone younger, he wouldn't have these struggles to have kids. As hard as it is to admit, the circumstances made me feel like less than a woman.

In the second, and final, round of in vitro, we implanted four embryos. I found out I was pregnant when I temporarily moved to Milford, Pennsylvania, to deal with Oliver during his troubling years away at school. I would drive to New Jersey from Milford to see a doctor. It was my weekly pilgrimage. One time, I had to take a flight to work in New York. My doctor wanted to make sure I didn't miss administering my daily shots in my stomach, so he armed me with a letter explaining why I would have vials of liquid and syringes in my carry-on bag. As I approached TSA, I was preparing my explanation and getting ready to pull out the official letter backing me up. Obviously, this was before 9/11, but they were still a red flag item to have in your carry-on. After my bag went through the TSA security scanner, I was not surprised that I got pulled to the side for what they saw. I saw the workers huddled at the screen looking at the image and calling co-workers over. I was ready for them. When the gentleman approached me I began by saying, "Oh, I have a letter from my doctor for the syringes and medicine."

They looked at me perplexed and said, "No, no, no, can you come and tell us what this is?" As they pointed to a long metal object in my bag, I couldn't help but laugh. The ticking time bomb in my belongings they were most worried about was nothing but a good, old-fashioned hot comb! Not the syringes, not the little nondescript vials. Go figure.

During the life-changing visit when I found out about my

pregnancy with my boys, I went into the room and the nurse said to me, "You're pregnant with twins and there's a 25 percent chance you will lose one of them." Just like that. Not an ounce of sugarcoating or lube. She dropped the news in a very matter-of-fact, raw way. I thought that was the most horrible thing any human being could say to someone. When I told my niece Marie the good news, she joked that if all four of them had took, she was going to leave town with no forwarding address! I appreciated her wit. She reminded me to keep laughing even in the most difficult of times.

Not only did my infertility teach me patience and resilience, through the process I also had to reinvent the way I saw my body, motherhood, and pregnancy in general. I had to push myself to so many limits that I never thought I would ever go to. As I mentioned before, this was a big reason I decided to pose for a *Playboy* magazine cover. I wanted to reclaim my power and honor my body even in the midst of what I thought was its betrayal. In my darkest days of struggle through infertility, I found myself growing bitter and envious of other pregnant women. I knew enough and believed enough in the power of energy to know that I had to change my mindset to change the outcome. I couldn't be jealous of other women who were pregnant. Putting thought into purpose, I switched it up. One of our friends, who's a big Hollywood manager, got pregnant, and I offered to throw her a big baby shower. Remember, I was still trying to get pregnant at the time. I threw myself into the projects and it turned out beautifully. It gave me purpose and allowed me to refocus my energy. To me, this was doing something good for both her and myself.

I was putting positive energy into the universe. Good begets good! Some might think it was like self-torture, but it was actually the best type of therapy. And that's resilience.

During my pregnancy, I was on edge once I realized that it was going to stick. We were beyond happy but still supercautious. We allowed ourselves to begin planning out the nursery, thinking of names, and other expectant parent tasks. I remember talking to my mom and being so excited to finally be able to share the pregnancy process with her.

As I progressed, I started to get these wicked headaches and noticed my blood pressure spiking. I called my doctor, and he told me to head to the hospital. When we got there, the doctor on call said, "I'm going to give you Vicodin." I thought, you're going to give me Vicodin, and I couldn't have coffee, wine, or eat sushi for the past few months? This freaked me out. Nonetheless, I ended up taking it, and an hour later, my headache was still there. "Did you have lunch?" the doctor asked, trying to troubleshoot. I confirmed that I did. With that, he said, "All right, we're taking out the babies tonight at eight o'clock."

I was panicked. All I kept saying was, "We're gonna have the babies so early! I'm only thirty-four weeks pregnant." I was devastated and immediately called my pediatrician, Dr. Peter Waldstein. I said, "Dr. Peter, they want to take out the twins tonight. It's too early!"

"What time?" he questioned.

"Eight o'clock and I'm scared," I said, sobbing.

"I'll be there." He reassured me. Sure enough, at seven o'clock, he walks into my room dressed in scrubs. "Your babies are going to be okay. Don't you worry," he promised. He was right there in the delivery room. Jax was the first one out and he was crying with such force. Hearing the healthy screams was one of the most amazing and gratifying sounds I've ever heard in my life, especially because I knew my journey. Mike was beaming with pride. Jaid followed right after. He wasn't crying and was very stoic and almost looked mad that we disturbed him. He was tough right from the start. Mike quickly left the room to accompany the babies for their birth checkup. I was still on the table pumped up on magnesium, which knocked me out completely. I didn't really get to see the boys again until the next morning. When they finally placed them in my arms, I never wanted to let go. It was a feeling like I never thought I would feel again. It was instant love. I was a new mom again. God heard my prayers.

My experiences have showed me that it's never too late for new beginnings. A profound trust in the ability of God paired with fearlessness, faith, fortitude, and a whole lot of false starts brought me to this place. Hitting my stride, defining my legacy, and finding my proverbial "G-spot" one trial at a time.

Five

Faith and Forgiveness: The Dark vs. The Light

Forgiveness does not
change the past, but
it does enlarge
the future.

—Paul Boese

Examining the very word "forgiveness" tells you all you will ever need to know about the act of forgiving: It's a gift to be GIVEN. It is the most liberating one you give to yourself. This is a lesson easy to understand but often hard to practice. Learning how to move forward, how to trust people, and how to relearn to rely on God were all crucial to my healing during the dark times throughout my life's journey.

One of my very first, and most memorable, incidents that challenged and schooled me on the art of forgiveness came at the hands of my absentee father. Axel Jean-Pierre was a hotfooted Haitian male. Like most Caribbean men of his generation, he was a stereotypical product of a hypersexual male culture: wild, fast, and in the streets, sowing his wild oats. I can't tell you how many times I would pretend I was asleep, only to creep out of my room to see my mom waiting until the wee hours just to get a glimpse of my father returning from an evening of Lord only knows what. Patiently, obediently, and faithfully, she waited. Never showing cracks of despair, sadness, longing, or lack. She waited and waited and waited. Waited for a man she knew never completely belonged to her. Waited for her deeply believed marriage vows to be honored and respected. Perhaps it was in those countless wee hours, peeping out of those well-worn drapes and lovingly tending to the dinner she kept warm, that she was building and nurturing her grace.

Time is a fleeting gift, and you never really know how long you have it for. One story of regret I live with is that I never sought to heal the wounds of my childhood when my mother was still alive. I was still paralyzed by the notion that a child never stepped out of line to question their parents' business. Grown folks' business. I wish I would have put away childish beliefs and asked her more questions about her journey as a woman. About her motivations and relationship with my father. I will never truly know what Marie

Claire Beauvais was thinking during those lonely nights, because I never asked. What I do know is that during my childhood, she never seemed bitter. Never hateful, or vengeful, and always there for us. In her quiet and dignified way, she taught me the powerful lessons of forgiveness and fortitude.

To be real, my mother was not a perfect woman, and neither am I. As a mother myself, I now realize that staying on that pedestal your kids put you on is a shaky foundation you're guaranteed to take a tumble from. It's not only guaranteed, it's also healthy.

Many years later, when I was a young adult, I found out that my father had written me a letter before he died. Because I had no direct relationship or contact with him as a young adult, he sent the letter to my mother to pass along to me. You remember when I said my mother was never bitter? Well, scratch that. I didn't find out about the letter until after he had passed away. What I also learned is that my mother threw it away without telling me, or allowing me to read it. Why she made this decision, you ask? I'm sure there's no straightforward answer. Partially, I think she thought she was protecting me. Mom knew how I felt and that I wanted nothing to do with my father. What is confirmed is that discarding his final message, and possibly his only real attempt at communication, impacted my life and sent me reeling in ways I never anticipated. I can't say that the letter would have absolved my father of the lingering results of his harshness and neglect. I can't say that it wouldn't have either. I can't confirm that it contained heartfelt apologies and multiple confessions of deep regret or undying love. I can't say it didn't either. What I can say is that the decision my mother made to destroy MY letter, regardless of her reasoning, was a selfish one. It was wrong. Not because KeKe wasn't entitled to her pain and anger—God knows she suffered—but it was wrong simply because she robbed me of my one and only chance to potentially ease some of my own pain. My mother, whom I cherished and adored, chose to fully participate in the pain and turmoil my father brought to her life. That was HER choice. I didn't get to make that choice. I was a kid. I will never know whether the "what ifs" would have been answered had I gotten to read his final letter to me. What I know is that in the absence of any type of official closure, it left me with a bunch of additional lingering questions.

For me, healing has been a conscious, dutiful exercise in strengthening my faith. I basically surrendered to God's plan. Everything happens for a reason. Understanding and accepting my parents as perfectly flawed people finding their way was an important first step. The golden ticket at the end of this journey was that forgiving my father and mother paved the way for me to forgive in other relationships. It also taught me how to take forgiveness inward and heal myself from my own mistakes and regrets. These have to be the greatest gifts I could've ever received.

Even while raising my own kids, I've had to practice forgiveness for both them and myself on a damn near daily basis. At times, I've completely lost my temper with my boys. The heat of anger does that to you. I'm sure even Mother Teresa herself let an f-bomb fly once or twice . . . well, maybe not. Thank goodness I don't claim to be Mother Teresa because I think it's healthy for your kids to see you lose it every now and then. It helps them to understand the concept of being human.

The lessons from my mother of regaining strength and powering through were my steadying rock when I faced one of the biggest emotional challenges of my life—my divorce from Mike Nilon. I thought I was done. We were supposed to grow old together.

The circumstances and reasons behind our divorce were messy and way too public. I wouldn't wish that experience on my worst enemy. My ability to trust and my faith in marriage took a beating along with confidence in my desirability as a woman. Faith, family, and friends saved me from the darkness. Coming to a place of acceptance was the first step for me. Acceptance of the death of what was, or what could have been. Acknowledgment of his role was easy, but my own role in arriving at that place was also crucial. Unpacking my hurt and anger to get to a place of forgiveness was not an easy journey, but I knew it was one I needed to take. I started seeing a therapist during my divorce. I mustered enough clarity to realize that I didn't want my children to bear the wreckage of our failed marriage or my toxic feelings of betrayal. Another goal of therapy was to find my way to a place where I could deal with Mike in my life, not as my husband. We both had to be available emotionally and physically to raise our boys. Basic questions as to whether I could even be in the same room with this man plagued my thoughts. I wanted to strangle him! How would I ever be able to put that aside and not disrespect him in the eyes of his boys, who still saw him as just Dad? He is a great dad but was a lousy husband. I had to learn how to separate the two.

Therapy works. It has done and continues to do wonders for me. In my hour of darkness and despair, my therapist challenged me to do a simple and seemingly irrelevant task. She said, "Do one of the things that scares you the most." At the time it seemed silly. I wasn't paying this woman all this money to develop a new hobby! She went on to explain that focusing on something that terrified me would allow me to get out of the negative headspace of my divorce. She said, "If you write with your right hand, switch to your left, because that'll force you to concentrate on something else. What task has scared you most?"

I replied, "I always wanted to write a children's book, but I don't know where to start. I don't even know if I can." With those very words, my next phase was hatched.

I was off on a new journey, and then fate stepped in to confirm I was on the right path. One day, I decided to take my energetic toddler sons to the park to blow off steam from being cooped up after a rare rainy day in LA. We arrived at the park, unloaded their toys, and they made a beeline straight to the only other kid in the park playing on the carousel. Naturally, when you're at the park and your kids are playing with other kids, you'd inevitably strike up a conversation with the other kids' parents. While standing at the edge of the apparatus area, I started making small talk with this guy who had a great British accent. We talked for about an hour and then finally I asked him, "What do you do for a living?"

He replied, "I own a comic book company. Actually, right now I'm focusing on building up my children's book division as well."

Ding, ding, ding! I immediately got chills and thought, *Okay, wow, that's God! This is not just a coincidence.* This guardian angel's name was Sebastian A. Jones. We exchanged information. And about a week later, I had a nagging thought that I had to follow through with my therapist's orders. This chance meeting was not just happenstance. The universe was speaking to me, and meeting Sebastian was no coincidence. So I called him and said, "Hey, it's Garcelle. I don't know if you remember me, but we met the other day in the park while our kids were playing together."

"Are you kidding me? he responded.

I chuckled and continued, "Well, I know you're starting your children's division of books and I wanted to run an idea by you. Can we meet up so we can discuss my idea?" When we finally connected, we spoke for hours about the possibilities and opportunities around what I was thinking. By the end of our conversation, we had struck a deal and decided to cowrite my children's books, the *I Am* series.

My original goal with the book was to work through my pain and come out on the other end whole. Once I gave voice to my nagging fear of authoring a book, I realized that I actually had a deep desire to create a safe space for kids and parents to ask questions and have dialogue around issues they were struggling to grasp. Having young biracial boys of my own, I wanted to arm them with knowledge about issues of self-awareness and race. Coming from a family of divorced parents brought an additional separate set of challenges and questions of its own. By giving them the language and tools early, they would be able to confidently confront any uncomfortable or hurtful situations that came up with their friends later on. In essence, I was healing myself and inoculating them at the same time.

Out of this divine collaboration, we came up with *I Am Mixed,* the first in our *I Am* book series, followed by *I Am Living in 2 Homes,* for children and parents who are dealing with divorce, and finally, *I Am Awesome,* to address issues of self-esteem in children at every level. With this leap of faith, I checked another item off my bucket list and was able to move on in my journey toward healing.

Ironically, my worst moments gave me the opportunity to relearn who I am and to appreciate my inner strength and ability to navigate any circumstance. Sometimes you forget how strong you can be until you are put in a situation where you have to carry yourself. I've grown, and the experiences of forgiving and rebuilding have given me the life I have today.

Bending to life's obstacles is key; breaking under them is not an option. I have too much to live for, be grateful for, and accomplish.

I believe the universe is filled with healing energies and messages all waiting for individuals to absorb. The messages can be seen, felt, and heard all around us if we are open to receiving them. I struggle sometimes to define my faith, which is definitely rooted more in spirituality as opposed to any one religion. I make this distinction because the personal relationship I have with God is paramount to my stability. Ever since early adulthood, I have separated the act of religiously going to church from the walk and intimate relationship

I have with my Creator. I thank God every day. I ask him for clarity, healing, strength, and redemption. Silently, inwardly, and through my actions, it's an ongoing exercise in faith. My innate awareness of and belief in universal forces have given birth to my love of natural stones and healing crystals. They are the most literal representations of the forces of nature. I have them everywhere in my home and draw strength and comfort from their presence. Other tools in my healing arsenal are candles and sage. The very word "sage" means wisdom and clarity, and that's what I feel it provides me with when needed. If I feel like things are a little off kilter in my life or feel off-balance, I light it up, meditate, and cleanse the energy around me. Similarly, I am never without scented candles burning at home and even on the road when I travel. There is something about the restorative and cleansing energy around fire that soothes me. The experience of beautiful scents calms my spirit and replenishes my soul.

Perhaps inadvertently, I have my Haitian roots to thank for my eclectic approach to spirituality. We're definitely a culture attuned with spiritual energy and forces. Even though, during my youth, the art of voodoo was not a practice in my household, I can't help but think it did enable me to believe in nature's powerful, lingering energy and forces more easily.

I am teaching my youngest boys the valuable gifts of nurturing spirituality and walking with God. Not in the regimented going to church every Sunday way that my mother instilled in me, but rather in a more holistic daily relationship and values sort of way. I want them to understand that God exists in every interaction and relationship they have, most of all with themselves. I want them to know that mirroring spirituality and the values associated with faith are crucial components for developing into their best selves as men. Living the walk, not merely talking the talk, is what counts most. As the saying goes, people may forget what you say, but they will never forget how you made them feel. Acts and words of service, kindness, and grace for others and themselves will be the greatest assets they can give.

In my journey, I've learned that in life you may get to choose whom you forgive, but you never get to choose why you forgive. It's really quite simple—we all forgive to move forward and to heal. Forgiveness is always the kindest and most liberating gift you can ever give to yourself. It frees up space in your head and heart so that you can allow other blessings, more bountiful blessings, to flow in. I challenge everyone to try it. You won't regret it.

Six

Finding My Voice While Black in Hollywood

When you own

your voice, you own

your power.

—Anonymous

I nsecurity coupled with the trappings of youth can be a hell of a thing. That's why we have intuition. I feel that we were given intuition to help guide us, especially when knowledge and experience are lacking. Not everyone is sensitive to this inner voice or trusts its validity; I do. It gives me courage and propels me to act in ways counter to what I would normally think of. I was raised by a mother who was deeply spiritually connected. I witnessed her uncanny ability to predict my response to situations based on a simple inflection in my voice or a peculiar expression on my face. To this day, I rely heavily on trust and listen to my gut. These have never failed me.

It's safe to say that, from a very young age, I've lived a very big and fast life. Jumping headfirst into living solo in a big city, international travel, and making lots of money allowed me to rub elbows with all kinds of people. During my early days in New York, once I was solidified as an up-and-coming model, I was getting calls from movie stars, TV stars, and millionaires inquiring about me and wanting to take me out. It was a mind-blowing experience for a young and impressionable girl who came from humble means.

On one particularly memorable day, I got a call from my agency saying that Bill Cosby wanted to have my phone number. To a young Black girl in the 1980s, that was a huge deal because he was one of the biggest celebrities and idols in Black pop culture. As a matter of fact, who didn't grow up knowing who Bill Cosby was, regardless of their background? Without even hesitating, I said yes, and my number was forwarded to him. Shortly after that, I got a small part on his hit sitcom *The Cosby Show*.

I was ecstatic! I played the nurse of Theo Huxtable's teacher, played by Sonia Braga, when she was having a baby. . . . I told you it was a small part! After rehearsals one evening, we got invited to accompany Mr. Cosby, in his limo, to meet up with a friend at the Park Avenue Hotel. Upon arriving at the hotel, we entered the private elevator to the penthouse suite. When the elevator door finally opened, to my surprise, the famous entertainer, singer, and comedian Sammy Davis Jr. was there waiting. I had to do everything to keep my jaw from hitting the floor! Flash forward and we were all casually sitting around in the living room talking and laughing as if we were all long-lost friends. As they traded funny stories about personal encounters, I couldn't help but hear the old *Sesame Street* lyrics "One of these things is not like the other" playing on repeat in my head. That thing, or person rather, was me! This was surreal. In my childlike mind, I was screaming that I was not worthy to be in the presence of such greatness. Who the hell did I think I was?

The next time Mr. Cosby invited me to his house was because he said he wanted to talk to me about going to college. His position was that he didn't want me to have to rely on modeling as my long-term career plan. He also mentioned that he planned to run through a couple of scenes with me when I got there. When I arrived at his impressive town house on the Upper East Side, I only saw Mr. Cosby. After a bit of time passed, I developed a nagging feeling that there was someone else in the house. Shrugging it off, I quickly decided that it was maybe just a butler, chef, or someone else who worked for him. I don't know why it bothered me, but I let it slide.

Mr. Cosby asked me if I wanted a drink, and for the first time I tried the famous sambuca. I can't remember if it had the coffee beans in it, but instantly I felt like a grown-up. Here I was, having a grown-up power meeting, all by myself, with a Hollywood icon—I had truly arrived! Taking a sip of the exotic concoction, I knew immediately I did not like it one bit! I have to admit, at the time, I wasn't a drinker at all.

Hell, I wasn't even of drinking age. On top of that, the nagging inner voice started to get louder and harder to avoid. I started to feel very uncomfortable for some reason. I don't know why, but something didn't feel quite right. I immediately made up an excuse and ran out of the town house like a bat out of hell. I was running from an unknown entity, and my sense of discomfort was all the jet fuel I needed.

I never saw Mr. Cosby again. He called, I never replied. If I recall correctly, it was the following week that he had his "I love my wife party." Aww . . . how quaint.

This was one of the first times I realized how important it was to trust my instincts and act on what I believed in, despite the situation. The power of my intuition is especially confirmed when I reflect on everything we've since learned about Mr. Cosby's predatory behavior. Even when his true nature was revealed to the world, I struggled inwardly with sharing my encounter because I didn't have any concrete allegations of impropriety. At the time, my soul spoke to me loud and clear. I had a feeling that things were on the wrong track, and in that moment, my gut saved me from confirming what could have become an awful reality. My gut, that bitch, has always known what's up even from early on. That's why she's been my number one ride-or-die until this day! Forsaking all others.

I thought I had made it. Not completely, to be honest, but at least I made it past the point of being a pushover in Hollywood. A successful model; check. I had a number one sitcom under my belt; check. Became a published author; check. Proved that I can hold my own in big-budget hit movies; check. Hell, I've even produced my own podcast from home during a pandemic (with the technological help of my son Jax), launched my own production company, and even occasionally put together my own IKEA furniture. I am every woman, damn it! But even though I've checked all these boxes in my career, I still face that never-ending struggle to prove and reprove myself over and over again. I call it the "pick me" syndrome. This is one of the sad realities in this business, especially for a Black woman in Hollywood. Is it me? Is it them? I lay awake at night sometimes agonizing over why, after all I have already accomplished, I still feel like I'm waiting for my big break.

Boy, have times changed! Take the daily breakdowns, put out on behalf of casting directors, which contained the current list of available roles in Hollywood projects. It was a meticulously detailed daily industry bible because it broke down the specific open casting needs of each ongoing production. From character type to body type, agents knew exactly who to send to any audition. For an overwhelmingly large majority of the productions, based on these predetermined roles, it was blatantly clear, project after project, that Blacks need not apply. Well, not unless you were aiming to be typecast as a thug, pimp, drug dealer, addict, or hooker. As a newer actress, I would get word from my agent that casting directors would say, "We are not going urban with this character. This is not a role for her." You read it right in their minds, the only type of Black roles they thought actors who looked like me were fit to play were "urban" ones. Translated as "stereotypically hood" ghetto ones. Not the part of judge, doctor, politician, astronaut, anxiety-riddled housewife; nothing. To casting directors, who are the gatekeepers of all acting jobs, there was room for only one Halle Berry in this business. For the rest of us, you better get in where you fit in. Don't get me wrong. Halle is a dear friend, and this has nothing to do with her acting ability. I use her name metaphorically only. This had to do with the narrowly confined categories we were forced into by the narrow lens of Hollywood. As a Black actor, you would just have to swallow the stinging rejection and say, "better luck next time." We'd been fed this same old lie and typecast negatively throughout history.

Whenever there was a role written for a Black actress, which were few and far between, we all ended up vying for the same part because we all knew another opportunity was not close behind. Oh, there were plenty of small bit roles such as strung-out junkie, ghetto sidepiece, or sassy friend, but hardly any that celebrated the strength and complexity of Black women. Please, we couldn't even dream of a role that would highlight us as just the girl next door; she was faithfully portrayed as white and far out of our reach. Competition was fierce in our community of actresses because sadly, everyone was just trying to work and grab a piece of the spotlight. Sure we had Diahann Carroll and Pam Grier to show the wide range of sex appeal and sophistication in the Black community, but they were anomalies rather than norms.

The party line that many power brokers in Hollywood would sell was the misconception that Black actors and actresses didn't pull in big money at box office. Well, *Black Panther* certainly shattered that myth, didn't it? Truth be told, in 1988, in my very first movie role, in *Coming to America*, the film proved that myth wasn't true either because it grossed a reported $350 million with a budget of only $36 million. Now, that's a box office success, not an anomaly.

In life, and especially in this profession, clearly racism is an unavoidable obstacle that Black actors don't have the luxury of saying, "No, I'm not interested. I'll pass on the dose of ignorance this time around. Thanks!" It's very much a practiced and unspoken price you have to pay for doing business in Hollywood. Some of the more popular cover-up phrases I've heard from casting directors are "We're not going Black with this character," or my favorite doozy, "This is not an urban story." I almost lost my mind when they dropped that one on me. Even though I knew this was a total snow job, like countless Black actors, I internalized it and thought there was something I was doing wrong or that I simply wasn't good enough.

It doesn't get any more generic than this role I was dying to read for centered around the concept of a recently widowed man who had suddenly lost his wife in a tragic accident. In the greatest act of unselfishness, his wife had opted to donate her organs after death. Fast forward a few years and the man now finds himself inexplicably drawn to a waitress whom he crosses paths with as she waits on him late one night. As you can guess, the mystery woman who the widower pursues for weeks ends up being the organ recipient of his late wife. A gripping story about loss, love, and redemption; sweet, right? Well, I thought it was a great role and couldn't have been more excited to read for it until I was denied a shot at even auditioning for the part.

The casting director for the movie diligently notified my agent, "We don't want this to be an interracial love story and we don't think the audience wants to see it told like that. Sorry!" Excuse me? Since when did love stories have any particular color to them? Maybe if we were still in Jim Crow days, but definitely not in a world where interracial relationships are seen in nearly every city in the world! This is the type of institutionally ingrained, small-minded bigotry that does not allow us to get further as a society when it comes to issues of race. The more stories that you see reflecting someone who looks like you, the more your image becomes an "acceptable" part of society. If I were the me I am today, I definitely would have called them out. "When you know better, you do better," as my friend in my head Maya Angelou says.

Thankfully, in today's Hollywood, I can say we are starting to crack that code of racism in casting. As actors and actresses of color we are finally breaking through to challenge the ideas of normalcy and rewriting stories that were being depicted only by actors who didn't look like me. Racist comments such as the ones that were made to me in the past would be like kerosene on a flame today. Today, I am different and so is the tolerance level in the broader world. Now that we are starting to see cracks in the ceiling when it comes to access and opportunities, we also have to ensure that we are getting our share when it comes to money.

Not so long ago, I played a part in a scripted drama in which I signed on for a recurring role. At the outset, the producer moaned about how the production didn't have a big budget, but they really thought I was "the one" they saw in this role. I was between jobs at the time, so the old flattery trick got me. After we started filming, they ended up treating me like a series regular, minus the compensation to back it up. I was written into almost every episode and had to fly cross-country to shoot. What's the problem with that? The money! I was being paid far, far less as a "recurring castmate" than they would have had to pay me if I signed on as a series regular. A whole lot less! That's bait and switch, and even as a seasoned professional in this business I fell for it. I know they wouldn't dare try to pull a stunt like this with Cameron Diaz, Drew Barrymore, Julianna Margulies, or any other of my white contemporaries. To make matters worse, I knew I was worth a higher deal than they had given me, but the problem was I didn't dig in and fight for it like I knew I was worth more. Point taken . . . lesson learned . . . G-spot reactivated!

Even when you are trying to create your own opportunities based on your own success, there are people who try to block your blessings. I collided head-on with this painful struggle a few months ago when I was up for a cohosting spot on a well-known Emmy Award-winning talk show that carried a three-year commitment with a pretty enticing financial incentive. As I said before, my philosophy is that I never turn down a meeting because you never know what could come out of it. To be honest, the journalism bug resurfaced for me in the past few years when I was up for a cohosting spot on both ABC's *The View* and CBS's *The Talk*. I consulted the "usual suspects" in my life and bounced my ideas and concerns off of them like I always do. It wasn't that I didn't think this was a good opportunity, but I was trying to piece it all together through the lens of being a CEO of my brand. Continuity is key for me. I had already set my sights on turning my name and lifestyle into a global brand, with many outlets, for my loyal fans to connect through. So, for me, it was more about making sure this opportunity was going to deliver that continuity with my future goals. Once I had decided to move forward, the pressure was on. This was a Thursday afternoon, and my screen test was the upcoming Monday. We were rocking and rolling, right? Well, so I thought.

The cat's out of the bag now; it's no secret that my big audition was for none other than the daytime talk show *The Real*. It's so ironic, I was hired by *The Real* to keep it real! It's what I do best. Looking back on it now, I was so frazzled, I didn't entirely process the enormity of the opportunity. It was all coming at me so fast, there was no time to psych myself out, get into my own head, and conjure those butterflies of nervousness. Monday came around quickly and I was prepared to give it everything I had. Even more importantly, I was in a place where I was comfortable showing up as my authentic self. Comfortable with my life lived to that point, accepting of most of my foibles and wrong turns, and more comfortable with expressing my opinions. I had a hunch this might be the time when all things work together in the great big universe to check this box off in my career and get the job. Prior to the audition, I had briefly met all the women a few times when I was a guest on the show promoting projects. They were all lovely. Each of them brought a little something different and unique to the conversation. As predicted, or as my gut was telling me, the audition went fan-flipping-tastic! We laughed, chatted about pop culture, and teased each other in a very playful and easy sort of way during the taping. They were all extremely welcoming and genuinely excited to have me join them at the table. I left the audition feeling like I had really found a space, and talk show opportunity, where I could be me. Where I would be valued.

Let me rewind to where I was with my other commitments. The ratings of my podcast *Going to Bed with Garcelle* were on the rise. I was awaiting my official contract for my second season of *The Real Housewives of Beverly Hills* (uh duh, I knew they weren't going to drop me), and I had a few other smaller projects I was in the process of pitching to various networks. To top it all off, I was planting seeds in the hopes of launching my beauty brand Garcelle Beauty and other lifestyle products. I had my hand in every cookie jar trying to come up with something extra sweet. That's the hustle. With all of those wonderful potential opportunities comes the sticky little obligation to sign contracts of commitment on the back end. Let's just say I was committed up the wazoo! None of that would have been an issue as long as I continued to deliver, on all of those projects, as I had been doing. Then came the opportunity for the cohosting gig, and shit began to unravel and people started to try to strong-arm situations.

Leading up to my decision to test for the cohosting spot on *The Real*, I had a conversation with an executive I was in contract with to do a development deal. I mean a real heavy hitter in the industry. He had already gotten wind that I was considering testing for the other gig. He went on to divulge that he didn't think it was a good move because he felt it was a step backward in my career. He suggested I hold out for my own talk show that he was *trying* to sell for the past year, but it hadn't sold yet. To paraphrase his words, "You are on the up-swing and I would hate for you to lock yourself into something that wasn't going to propel you forward." On its face, that seemed reasonable to me, but I still wasn't sold on that line of thinking. Now, instead of being thrilled about the opportunity to be a part of an Emmy Award–winning cast, I was starting to doubt if it was for me. After all, I trusted his advice and opinion completely. To be clear, being in a talk show seat was on the top of my bucket list; now I was second-guessing when a real opportunity was presented. Crazy!

My heart sank when my manager, Gordon, confessed that the only way the executive would clear me to test for the cohosting spot, because I was already contracted with him, was if the ma-jor network for that show agreed to be in fourth position. Now, for those who aren't in "the business," accepting a fourth option spot is like being the backup dancer to the backup dancer's dog walker. No shade to dog walkers and backup dancers out there, but you get my drift. There is no damn way any major network would agree to come in fourth place, in terms of priority for projects, if they were signing new talent to a lucrative three-year deal. No way. Not going to happen, and he had to have known that.

To be clear and completely transparent, I know that he had my back and believed in my ultimate dream of titling my own talk show. He wanted the best for me and was pushing so hard to make it come to fruition. I think the part that bothered me the most was I felt it was a power move. The opportunity with *The Real* was real and here now. Why wouldn't I jump on that? Who knows when another studio would come calling and green-light my own talk show? Please don't try to block me from a potentially sure thing! This had zero to do with my ability to deliver and meet the challenge because I was successfully meeting all my other obligations. Never once did I indicate that I wasn't going to give each project 110 percent of my effort, even if I had to catch a catnap between wardrobe changes. I never do anything halfway. When I commit, I commit fully. I take professionalism very seriously and have always prided myself on showing up ready and prepared. I was definitely frustrated. This is the "sausage making" part of the business that's always a little messy. I'm so glad I kept my cool and practiced patience.

Everything worked out in the end; thank God for compromise, lawyers, and my team, Gordon Gilbertson, Babette Perry, Mark Johnson, and Steve Muller. I'm glad I stuck to my guns and fought for *The Real* gig. That feeling that I was worth fighting for. It was my time to assert myself, not revert to accepting what was given to me. This was the exact type of instance I needed to remember my worth, remind people of it, and dig in and fight. The remarkable thing about true value is that it never diminishes, no matter how much it gets dinged up.

Once settled into *The Real*, I felt vindication for my decision. The viewing audience seemed to really appreciate and like what I had to bring to the table. We all click so well together and have so much fun engaging in thoughtful conversations and grilling our guests. Especially the cute ones. And because it was during the time when Black

Lives Matter issues were dominating the world's attention, we got to have really transformative in-depth conversations with guests such as vice presidential candidate Kamala Harris, Chelsea Clinton, and Stacey Abrams. It was incredible to be able to have these conversations without any judgment. Mind you, because of COVID-19, during my first season on the show we never actually had the opportunity to be in studio together since I signed on. When the synergy works, it works. During the first season from our neatly decorated little home studios, Loni Love, Adrienne Houghton, Jeannie Mai-Jenkins, and I had a virtual girl's party every episode. It honestly doesn't even feel like work; well, maybe except on the days when we shot three episodes back to back. Whew! I am so proud of what we were able to do given the uncertainty in the world, inevitable technical glitches, and logistical pitfalls. First year down and we shot a whopping 170 episodes in eight months. Time flies when you're having fun. That's a whole lot of hair, makeup, wardrobe, and talking. I actually didn't even want to hear my own voice on some days. Now, that's girl power.

Life teaches you that pause time is your breathing space to reevaluate a situation and gather facts. Sort of like a fitting room for potential opportunities. The gap time in which you can spin, and turn in your mind, and look at the opportunity from every angle to make sure it fits you properly. Before you actually sign on the dotted line. In these moments of pause I reassert my worth, not find it.

I now confidently speak my truth, act on it, and voice my ideas. I do these more freely with the understanding that my voice matters too.

Seven

My Village

People come into your
life for a reason,
a season, or a lifetime.
When you figure out
which one it is, you will
know what to do for
each person.

—Unknown

Before there were my friends, there was my family. As I mentioned before, I credit my older sisters Yves-Rose, Carole, Gladys, and Chantal with teaching me how to step into the gap. How to be there in a pinch and pick up the slack when duty calls. They showed me the significance of sisterhood. They exemplified what it means to show up when life circumstances demand, even if you don't feel ready or capable.

I have met a lot of people in my lifetime but have very few close friends. Friendships come in many forms and serve a multitude of purposes in my life. I have many acquaintances whom I run into periodically or see every so often. We genuinely have a great time when we get together, but for some reason, we don't end up staying in close contact. I also have countless people I've worked with on projects. Through the sheer amount of time you spend at work, you inevitably get close to people and develop bonds. Sometimes they even become lifelong friendships long after the job is done. Then there are your partners in crime. The group you know to call when you want to do very specific things. Clubbing, going on vacation, pure debauchery. This is the fast and fun group that's always ready for a good time. And then, if you're *really* lucky, you have your front row. I heard this expression once in reference to your core group of supporters who are always there for you. The term resonated with me and seared itself deeply into my psyche, becoming my own life motto. It was the perfect phrase to describe my friends who'd seen me at my ugliest and who know way too damn much about my life. You can call on these gems for anything at any time and they're always present. They are the family you choose, whether or not there's any familial relation. My front row keeps me honest and makes me whole.

In my mind, one friend isn't supposed to fulfill every aspect of friendship. Each friend gives me a little piece of something, which adds up to a whole lot of medicine for my soul. Despite being blessed with millions of people who connect with me through my body of work, I still only have a small circle of people I call my true friends. This is definitely one instance where I'll gladly take smaller any day!

Sometimes you are the one who needs to save your friend. How do you navigate the space between crossing the line and being effective as a good friend? I once had a friend named Paula Barbieri. Yes, that Paula. Like, the one who dated O. J. Simpson Paula. Anyway, when I moved to Los Angeles, we started modeling a lot together. We hit it off instantly because we had similar dreams of success and similar personalities. We were street savvy and focused on making it. She kept on talking about her boyfriend. Everything she said consisted of "My boyfriend this. My boyfriend that." You know how it goes when someone mentions something so much, in such vague terms, the mounting intrigue kind of forces you to ask the next inevitable question, who's this boyfriend you keep mentioning? After taking the bait and asking, I came to find out that her elusive fellow was none other than O. J. Simpson himself.

One day, Paula FedExed me a fancy invitation to his birthday party. I was still wet behind the ears and had never gotten an invitation via FedEx before. It was going to be my and Danny's first "Hollywood party," and it was a big deal for me. When we got to O. J.'s house in Brentwood, where the party was held, and pulled up to the valet, I was instantly impressed with the drama of it all. As an attendant opened the car door, an elegant tray of champagne was presented to us. Perfection! The epitome of Hollywood glamour. We slowly made our way through the party, on the tennis court, which had been magically transformed into an elegant event space. Crossing over a little bridge, we realized that a beautiful rambling pool ran underneath. I remember finding out at the end of the night that O. J. had a young daughter who had tragically drowned in that very same swimming pool. My first thought was, *If you could afford to move, why would you choose to stay in a home where your child had drowned?* I can't lie, I found it a bit weird at the time, but *mind your business, Garcelle . . . mind your business!*

Soon after the party, O. J. became a more visible fixture in Paula's life. He would come to many photoshoots and have lunch with us during our breaks. He was naturally charming, funny, and easily won everyone over. He was O. J. Simpson the icon, for goodness sake. We were all mesmerized by how "lucky" Paula seemed to be.

I remember one eerie day Paula called me at home and she didn't sound like she was in good spirits. "Is everything okay? Are you okay?" I asked a little hesitantly.

"I just had a huge fight with O. J. He kicked me out of a car while we were on the highway." She continued to confide hesitantly. Then she asked me a question that haunts me to this day. She said, "Has Danny ever threatened you? Like, I mean said he could kill you?"

I was stunned and taken aback by the question and nervously laughed it off by saying, "No, don't be silly." She didn't say anything more, and the awkward silence kind of hung in the air between us. It wasn't exactly shocking to me because I was aware that they had a very turbulent kind of relationship, but the comment still left me a little unsettled. Judging by her initial demeanor, I could tell it gave her the same feeling.

Very soon after, O. J. Simpson was a suspect in the infamous Nicole Brown Simpson murder case. One day, I turned on the news and saw my friend Paula testifying in court in the high-profile case. I also discovered she had packed up and moved to Florida. Who knows what kind of hell she had gone through during her time dating O. J.? I can't say I confronted her again about the question she had once asked me, or her relationship volatility. I think I avoided the topic partly because it made me really uncomfortable and I had no idea what to tell her to do. Paula seemed totally enamored with him, and he was always so suave, jovial, and debonair. He had us all fooled, I guess. If I could go back and educate the younger me, I would tell myself that her friend Paula had been crying out for help. I should have followed up and taken it more seriously. Not saying it would have changed anything, I realize that, but it couldn't have been easy for her to share such a dark truth with me either.

Being an actress in Hollywood adds an extra layer to the concept of friendship, which is already extremely complex on its own. For me personally, the privacy aspect has a lot to do with it. I learned the hard way that you have to be extremely cautious about who you let into your inner circle. Listen, let's be real. *Page Six*, *TMZ*, and *Media Takeout* don't come up with all their celebrity dirt out of thin air. The best remedy for not getting caught out there is to have a strong coalition of those ride-or-die friends who keep your butt out of the tabloids.

I distinctly remember my invitation to the premiere of the block-buster *Miami Vice* movie starring Jamie Foxx and Colin Farrell. It was supposed to be a big red-carpet moment for me, because I had a few new projects in the works, and the movie itself had a huge buzz around it for obvious reasons. The added publicity attached to at-tending such an event was huge. To say I was ready was an under-statement; I was bringing my A game in the wardrobe department. A gorgeous Azzedine Alaïa bodycon leopard print dress, sleek bounc-ing and behaving bob hairstyle, with killer four-inch Louboutins. All of this packed into a size four frame that had been on a diet for the past two weeks to make this a headline night. I was ready to own the red carpet, honey!

Everyone who was anyone was there and all eyes were on this highly anticipated movie. Before the night got under way, my crew of girlfriends, who were my plus ones, joined me as invited guests at Jamie Foxx's pre-event cocktail party that everyone who was anyone was going to. We were a striking bunch. Tall, stacked, curvy, and fine as hell . . . my sassy crew was definitely a sight to behold. As the pre-game party went on, we were having a blast throwing back shot after shot of tequila. After an hour, we skipped to the awaiting stretched limo and giggled our way to the main event, which was about a mile away. Lipstick check, quick underarm spritz, boobs forward, and out the limo, I sprang to the screams from thousands of amped-up fans and a dizzying stream of lights and flashes. I had arrived! After three quick little uneven shuffled steps, I knew something wasn't quite right; I wasn't quite right. My girls were stumbling behind me, but a little steadier on their feet than I was. You know the feeling when you know you're drunk but you overcorrect to cover up? I was a pretty hot mess! I pulled myself together like a trooper and made a beeline to the step-and-repeat. Breezed through the interview line cackling freely with reporters while throwing my head back in uncontrollable laughter at the stories I was telling. I was clearly feeling myself and very impressed with my own performance. I turned to the left, turned to the right, flung my hair, and batted my eyelashes. . . . I was serving it all up.

After finishing my last interview, I met my girls and press agent at the end of the press line. The look on their faces was that of concern. Someone quickly shoved a glass of water in my hands and I was being whisked away all too quickly to a small corner of the outdoor event space. Things began to get a little fuzzy, and trails of sweat began to run between my cleavage. Oh no, I was about to black the fuck out!

I swear I only closed my eyes for a hot minute, but when I reopened them, chaos had ensued. I was down on the floor. Two of my girls were standing over me and straddling my body to shield me from the cameras. My PR angel and security were pushing people back and my other girls were frantically fanning me. My sophisticated bob was now a disheveled heap on my head. My mascara was streaming down my face, and one of my eyelashes was plastered to my left boob. My once sexy bodycon dress was now a tube top up around my waist. I was totally ass out, literally and physically. It was an epic fail and it was about to be an epic disaster in the media if my friends and team hadn't stepped in and quashed it. That's what your ride-or-die squad is for; they provide cover when you need it!

Talk about having my back. I had two friends, in their twenties, who rolled up unannounced to the house of this guy I had been dating. "Trevor" (Hollywood actor) had been a quick little relationship stopover for me, but it was a relationship full of nonstop arguments and stress. We would clash over everything. I think he was actually a sex addict. He would pull out his penis everywhere we went. Like an on-demand service. Hell, he'd do it even when there was no demand at all. He just liked to constantly air it out, I guess. Hmm, that should have been a sign to run the other way. It was a Friday evening and I had told my girls I was headed out to his apartment to possibly end things with him. After not hearing from me for a few hours, those girls got out of their beds at 3:00 a.m. and trekked all the way to his place in Hollywood. Oh, and one of them showed up packing a pistol in her panties just in case things got out of hand. Yeah, I got some gangstas residing in my reserved section up front too!

There's no rhyme or reason to how and when you make these close friendships. They are bonds that form in situations you least expect: school, work, at a party, the nail salon. One memorable moment where I found true sisterhood was on set while filming the *Girlfriends' Getaway* movie in Trinidad. It was really like the utopia of road maps for how working relationships should be in Hollywood. Myself and three other confident, accomplished, and professional women (Terri Vaughn, Melinda Williams, and Essence Atkins), all bringing their unique talents together to create onscreen magic. No drama, one-upmanship, fighting, or backstabbing. Perhaps it was because we were an all-Black cast and had such synergy in terms of life experiences. We knew each other and we were comfortable being ourselves without having to explain who we were. Kudos to the producers and director, because they created an environment of equality among contemporaries. All of the ladies had identical-size hotel rooms and in-depth story-line development; we were all there to do a job as peers. Those simple details matter and they definitely set the tone for a production. Even to this day, we love seeing each other and reconnecting.

Friendship and relationships of any kind are hard work. The very root of the word "relationship" means you have to relate, connect, and identify with someone else. The younger me often believed, with *any* relationship, you get what you put in. If you were attentive and present, this would usually create harmony and togetherness. If you were loyal, that would produce loyalty. As I said, this was the younger version of myself. Through life experiences I've learned that relationships and friendships are more complicated and nuanced than that. Good intentions sometimes get clouded by bad judgment, and loyalty for a friend sometimes gets put on the back burner for loyalty to family.

I remember I had a very dear friend during my second marriage who was like a sister to me. We genuinely had a bond that surpassed just the surface details. We spent hours laughing and joking with each other. We shared similar viewpoints and a love for having fun. Our paths in life seemed to coincide, with she and I sharing the joys of pregnancy at the same time. My husband was very close with her husband, which was a win, because my husband didn't keep many friends. I let her into my world, and she shared hers with me. We were always there for each other through all the ups and downs.

Upon coming to terms with the fact that my marriage was ending, I would initially cry to her and expose my raw emotions of anger, frustration, and fear. In the beginning, she would listen and say that everything was going to be okay. That initial understanding and comforting sisterhood soon gave way to distance and silence as she began to pull away, extracting herself from our friendship and eventually my life. We never had an argument, nor did we have any messy drama. Poof! She just disappeared. What I soon learned was that she sided with my ex-husband in our breakup. Not that she told me so; she just stopped being there for me as a true friend should. She chose loyalty to her husband, who was still friends with my ex-husband, over our friendship. Initially, I was devastated and deeply hurt by what she had done; she had broken the unwritten rules of the "girl code."

The "girl code" varies slightly for everyone. In general, it's an unspoken road map to building healthy relationships among women. Don't date each other's men. Don't let a man come between you and your girls. Don't betray each other's trust. Be that shoulder of support during a breakup . . . the list goes on and on. Basically, be a real fucking friend, not a stale-ass bitch!

Needless to say, that "friend" was ushered to my nosebleed section, and observes my life from the bleacher seats now, or through Facebook and Instagram.

How do I know my front row? Well, it's less about what I know and more about how each person in my front row makes me feel. I'm very in tune with the energy that people give off in general. Character and truth are everything to me. I need them from my close friends in good times and bad. When I want to hear them and even when I don't. Correction, especially when I don't. Keeping it real, I love my fans dearly, but I don't need fans as friends. (Please read the previous sentence twice.) It's not that we don't sing each other's praises, because we do. What we don't do is put each other on top of unrealistic pedestals that are impossible to maintain. As women we do a good enough job beating up on ourselves without help. We are real with each other even when real is not really pretty. My front-row people are the ones I can be vulnerable with and expose my unvarnished self to. No holds barred; they are strong women who don't take any bullshit, not even from me. They are their own people, with their own lives, talents, and successes. Some party hard with me; others shop just as hard with me. Some have my back in business ventures and parenting fails, and others keep my life organized and moving forward. To them, I am just Garcelle.

My girl code for my front-row hustlers is simple. We need to be there for each other. It's not transactional by any means, but for me, friendship without intentional participation is just lip service. Anyone who really knows me can attest, I've never been one to do fillers—of *any* kind!

Eight

Reality Bites: Behind-the-Scenes Stories

I am the master of
my fate and the captain
of my destiny.

—Nelson Mandela

M y ability to be self-sufficient has served me well while staying
relevant in the wacky, fickle world known as Hollywood. In
the beginning, ignorance was my greatest asset as an actor because
I had no idea how "the business" worked. There were no inner rules

of "usual business norms" telling me what I could and couldn't do, so I did everything the way I wanted to. One of my first serious acting gigs was on a show called *Models Inc.* and it too came to be because I persisted and found a way to turn a no into a yes.

It was 1993, and I was going back and forth from LA to New York while juggling modeling jobs, because that's how I was making my bread and butter at the time. My agent had mentioned to me that he had heard they would be holding auditions for a new show about models and the modeling scene. He said he'd look into it and let me know if there was any interest in me auditioning for a part. The initial plot had me intrigued. I had a hunch I'd be perfect for a role on that show because, quite frankly, it was so similar to my real life. A few weeks went by and I hadn't heard anything more about auditioning, so I phoned my agent.

"Hey! Whatever happened to that modeling show that you were looking into for me?" I inquired.

My agent responds, "Oh, they decided they're not going to hire any Black models."

I found this statement really weird because it was supposed to be a dramatic series about the trials and tribulations of young models competing in an elite modeling agency. How can this be? I know there weren't a whole bunch of us who had broken through the color barrier in the elite world of modeling, but DAMN! What about the Beverly Johnsons, Imans, and Naomi Campbells of the world? I was livid! We existed whether they liked it or not! I dreamed that night that I was talking to the creator of the new show, Mr. Aaron Spelling.

Was this my Haitian intuition kicking in? I woke up the next morning on a mission. I never mentioned anything to Danny, whom I was married to at the time, and decided to find out where the office of Aaron Spelling is. Remember, this was way before Google or Siri, so I had to do some real digging. I'll never forget how excited I was when I finally discovered that the office address was 5757 Wilshire Boulevard, in Los Angeles. Propelled by the dream about meeting Aaron Spelling, whom I had never met before, I decided to act on this newly discovered info. Not wasting any time, I wrote him a letter saying why I thought I should be in his new modeling show. That night, I packaged together some modeling pictures and a résumé and decided to hand-deliver them to him the next day. Obviously, these were the good old days before 9/11 changed the world with complicated security protocols. The next morning, I walked into his office and realized that the receptionist was a Black girl. This gave me a bit of comfort because I felt like I could strike up a conversation and build instant camaraderie. I said, "Hi, I'd like to see Mr. Spelling, please."

"Do you have an appointment?" she asked, looking at me through squinty eyes with her head tilted to the side.

I said, "Um, well, no, I don't. But if he can see me, that'll be great."

She chuckled and shook her head and said, "Well, it doesn't work like that. You need to have an appointment to see Mr. Spelling. I'm sorry."

Not being discouraged by her response I continued, "Well, do you mind if I leave a package for him with you?"

"What's in the package?" she questioned, giving me a half smile.

I said confidently, "It has modeling pictures of me and a letter saying why I think I should be part of his new show about models." I really don't know what I said to win her over, but she promised she would personally hand it to Mr. Spelling when she saw him. Never one to let grass grow under my feet, I called the receptionist the next day and quizzed her about whether she had handed the package to him, and she said YES!

About three days later, I got a call from Mr. Spelling's office. I had gotten an audition with the casting director of the show. I was ecstatic! Four days later, I was reading in front of Aaron Spelling himself and landed the role as Cynthia Nichols on *Models Inc.* She was featured as a troubled yet confident African American model. I appeared in twenty-five episodes in the first, and only, season that the show lasted. Who knows if Cynthia Nichols was originally supposed to be cast as a Black character, but she was now! Self-advocacy and persistence, I tell ya! Never underestimate the power of either.

I took my modeling portfolio one step further in 2006 when I made the monumental power move and posed for *Playboy* magazine. Let me clarify why I did it, especially in spite of sporting estrogen patches on my belly from fertility treatments that had to be artfully airbrushed out. It wasn't a vanity project for me to prove that I looked good naked. It was more of a milestone marker in my evolution toward self-acceptance. I was forty and about to be the cover girl for the August 2007 issue of *Playboy*. I am immensely proud of how the pictures turned out. Unfortunately, at the time, *Playboy* didn't normally offer their cover position to many Black women, so this was major

Me and Mommy.

Where my love of dance started.

Bundled up in Boston.

My only Christmas with my dad.

Standing out in my group of friends.

Having Oliver at such a young age helped
redefine and shape my life. He is my joy.

My miracle twins, Jax and Jaid Nilon,
were born October 18, 2007.

Keeping life normal after the divorce.
Holding on tight.

Feeding the homeless at the LA Mission.

Recent family photo. *From left:* Jax, me, Jaid, Oliver, and my first grandbaby, Oliver Jr. They are all the reason I do what I do. This is my heart.

Danny, Oliver, and me.

My niece Marie always had such a special bond with Oliver.

Mom loved to dance. I get it from my mamma.

A united family front. In Colorado to pick up Oliver from his treatment facility.

Strong and resilient women reside in my family.
From left: Marie-Flore Beaubien (niece), Yves-Rose, me, Carole, my sister Chantal.
Bottom center: Natasha DesRuisseaux (niece).

I'm so proud of the father Oliver has become.

Sisters.

Mike and I during our marriage, in happier times. I thought he was my forever love.

One of the reasons I fell in love with Mike was because he fully embraced Oliver as his own.

Jaid, Mike, and Jax.

My friend Paula Barbieri, pictured here (*left*) with my sister Yves-Rose.

It was one of the best times of my life being in Luther Vandross's *Take You Out* video.

Celebrating my brother from another mother, Jamie Foxx, on this 2005 Oscar win.

Halle Berry attending my *I Am* children's book launch. Who says women in Hollywood don't support each other?

Michael Jordan and me.

It's good to know fashion icons, especially when they are this hot! Tom Ford and me.

GARCELLE

GARCELLE

HEIGHT: 5'8½" BUST: 34C WAIST: 23 HIPS: 34 SIZE: 4-6 HAIR: DK.BROWN EYES: BROWN

My first modeling comp card, when I signed with Ford Models.

My very first *Essence* magazine cover, from August 1981. Being discovered on a city bus by Suzanne L. Taylor and then landing my first *Essence* cover solidified that my move to New York was the right one.

Bunny Garcelle reporting for duty.

BOOM! That's all, folks.

GARCELLE
BEAUVAIS
When it comes to staying beautiful, the actress doesn't discount the power of having good genes. "It's 80 percent of it, and the rest is how I take care of it," says Beauvais, who's currently starring in the film *Small Time.* "I have eczema, so I'm really on top of my skin in terms of moisturizing. I also try to eat healthy, but I'm not crazy about it," says the mom of three (including 6-year-old twin boys, Jax and Jaid). "If I'm with my kids and it's pizza night, I am having a couple pieces for sure!" As for exercise, Beauvais—who does Pilates and runs on a treadmill— came up with a routine that fits perfectly into her busy life. "I joined a gym right next to my kids' school," she says. "So I can drop them off and then have no excuse."

People magazine.

Coming to America (1988) was an epic entry into Hollywood for me. Then to follow it up thirty-three years later and be invited to reprise my role in the sequel *Coming 2 America* (2021)—a complete mic drop moment for me!

Finding the story of *LALO's House* was fate. Working alongside the film's young creator, Kelley Kali, and co-executive-producing this work as the first project under the Beauvais Wilson Productions umbrella was an honor. My partner Lisa L. Wilson and I were humbled, enlightened, and found new purpose.

During my weeklong audition for a cohosting spot at *The View*.

I took a "real" leap of faith when I signed on to be the first Black housewife on *The Real Housewives of Beverly Hills* franchise. I'm glad I did.

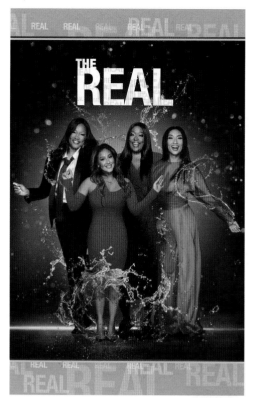

My talk show dreams were finally realized in 2020 when I joined as cohost of the award-winning daytime show *The Real.*

© Warner Bros. Unscripted Television/ Telepictures Productions.

Making my appearance on *The Cosby Show* when I was a young model.

Humanitarian work in
my homeland of Haiti.

Some of my village.
From left: Nicole E. Smith,
Whitney Pavlik, Tahiese
"Tazz" Beckford, Sagine
Archer.

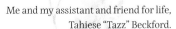

Me and my assistant and friend for life,
Tahiese "Tazz" Beckford.

for me. The photos were done on my own terms, and I respected the *Playboy* team for giving me the creative liberty to choose the photographer and dictate my level of comfort with what "baring it all" meant. They even gave me location selection rights. Anywhere in the world I wanted to shoot. Wouldn't you know it? I chose the *Queen Mary* in Long Beach, California. Exotic, right? Side note: I had to stay close to home for my regimented doctor appointments. Back to the story. I clearly didn't do my homework thoroughly because I found out later that the boat was haunted. I didn't sleep a wink the night before the big shoot, trust me.

At the time, I was incredibly self-conscious of my body because I was still in the headspace of the high-fashion modeling world, where thin enough was never thin enough. Such a complete 180-degree turn from hating my skinniness as a child. I was also about to turn forty-one and trying to get pregnant. On top of that, I was a Black woman competing against the norms of what was seen as beautiful in America. I was definitively Black, not mixed or an exotic mélange of races. I was already a mother as well. A young mother who had quickly regained her pre-baby body, but a mother nonetheless. Mothers were not typically regarded as sexy . . . not where I came from. I'm not sure how successful the issue was in terms of circulation numbers, but even more importantly, it was a personal triumph. The finished photos were pretty good, if I do say so myself. I might even have to admit to myself that they were HOT! I was proud that they were styled in a very artistic and sophisticated way that didn't scream trashy or sleazy. I was desperately hoping for this. Perhaps the last, and possibly best, gift my mother ever gave me was her response to the photos. She was supportive as hell and my biggest cheerleader. So opposite of what you would think an old-school West Indian mother would, or "should," be like. "If I had a body like that, I would have done the same thing!" Those were her words to me. It wasn't that I was shocked by her response. It was more that I was pleasantly surprised by it. She saw me for who I was; she always had. She also saw me for the woman I had become and was proud of that too. Soon after the *Playboy* issue was released and my twins were born, she passed away.

The Jamie Foxx Show (1996–2001) has become one of the most memorable ensemble cast I've acted in to date. I was Francesca "Fancy" Monroe, costarring opposite the charmingly hilarious comedian Jamie Foxx. For five amazing years, we were a runaway hit for the newly formed WB Network, chalking up a hundred unpredictably iconic episodes.

What started out as a loosely based autobiographical spin on Jamie's rise to fame became a cultural treasure for the Black community. The plot was about Jamie reluctantly joining his family's hotel business because he was new to Los Angeles and trying to get his singing career off the ground. The King's Tower Hotel, owned by his aunt Helen and uncle Junior King, played by Ellia English and the veteran comedian Garrett Morris, was the scene of daily hijinks. I played the beautiful and smart front-desk receptionist and the object of Jamie's goofy, nonstop romantic pursuit. Keeping the whole ship above water was Braxton P. Hartnabrig, played by

Christopher B. Duncan. He was the money man and stereotypical uptight accountant and Jamie's built-in punching bag. Some people tuned in to see Jamie's crazy slapstick comedy style or the King's entrepreneurial shenanigans. Others watched to gawk at my micromini uniform skirt, or laugh at Braxton's awkward fits of anger. Whatever the reasons, viewers tuned in faithfully. *The Jamie Foxx Show* had a fun and loyal fan base that we truly appreciated. We never took for granted that we were one of a small handful of Black-centric shows on television at the time. We depicted our people as business owners. We showed the ups and downs of young Black men and women trying to find love, work, and progress in their careers. We celebrated Black women as sexy and objects of desire, not as just the help. We highlighted characters' everyday struggles to get through life minus the stereotypical drugs and shooting scenarios, things that white shows never had the burden of balancing. On top of it all, we provided a safe space for our audience to laugh at unique cultural differences as well. I'd like to think we made a little impact within society without people even realizing they were being affected.

A little harmless flirtation never hurt anyone either. Jamie and I had an undeniable chemistry that definitely translated well on camera. I will even confess that we shared a steamy kiss once backstage. There was nothing brotherly about that one! Maybe in a different time and space and under different circumstances . . . after all, he is definitely very handsome and a real charmer. He was easy to get along with and easy to love. Because we realized early on that we had created something special with *The Jamie Foxx Show*, literally magic in a bottle, we decided not to mess it up with a real-life relationship. We were there to do a job and do it well. We were both professionals who took our silly job seriously. He became like my brother from another mother, my protector and mentor. Even though we were like family, I must confess that I did catch a glimpse of Jamie naked once. Let's just say that his tool belt was pretty stacked! He might have had enough tools for two jobs actually. Girl, I can't lie, seeing "the full scope" of what he was working with in that department kind of put the fear of God in me as well.

Recently, Jamie and I had a chance to catch up and chat candidly on my *Going to Bed with Garcelle* podcast. Needless to say, it was nonstop belly laughs punctuated by a whole bunch of NC-17 language. We talked about dating while famous and the loneliness and isolation that being a celebrity often brings. Jamie confessed that there were many emotions attached to being a celebrity that people don't understand. I shared with Jamie that earlier in my career he had once given me some of the best advice I've ever gotten about dating in Hollywood. When I was in the midst of my first divorce, Jamie told me that I should always remember to leave a little love for myself and not to give it all away. I have carried this nugget of wisdom with me ever since. Jamie would always say people would ask him if I had changed with the shine of the spotlight and success. His reply would always be the same: "I always waited for her to change, but she never did!"

We shared stories about the unrealistic notions that people tend to think that celebrities are not susceptible to humanlike emotions, insecurities, or needs. What more could we want, or need? We have money and fame, right? It's a false belief that money has made us abandon who we are as people. That we couldn't possibly need any of the basics that make everyone human. The things we strive for most in life—love, understanding, compassion, acceptance—can't be bought. I guess you can say it's one of the prices you have to pay for being a celebrity; one that I'm sure almost every one of us would trade in a New York minute.

Both single at the time, we also chatted about how COVID-19 has pushed us to our limit. We bantered back and forth about having to tap into our creative side both in finding ways to please ourselves physically, if you get my drift, and stimulating our professional sides as well. Hatching new show ideas, launching new business ventures, and creating content and platforms to elevate other Black creatives in Hollywood and beyond. And yes, we flirted with the idea of reuniting our characters Jamie and Fancy to complete their story and see where life took them. Even until this day, the nostalgia for *The Jamie Foxx Show* lingers. We both agreed that, given the right scenario, we'd both be down for it. Everyone wants to see what became of Fancy and Jamie. I say, stay tuned!

One of the greatest myths about being a celebrity is that you're always in demand and always working. In reality, being an actor is like being a glorified intern. Every few weeks, you're a newbie on the job and learning about a new cast, new director, and new producer. You definitely have to be okay with uncertainty and change to last in this business. The ability to accept rejection and disappointment is baked in. You always have to prepare yourself to hear the reasons why you aren't good enough to make the cut. I guess there should be no surprise as to why many of us suffer with issues of insecurity and a persistent need for reassurance. Our lives are ruled by continual critique, so after a while, you can't help but internalize some of it. Even the strongest and most grounded among us succumb to the darkness at times.

In the early days, and sometimes even now, I've had to fight to break out of the narrow mold that casting directors, agents, and even fans wanted to put me in. I've never been just a model, or just an actress. By nature I am always looking for ways to stretch myself and add depth to my list of talents and skills. Ironically, the mountain of change that I had to endure from an early age prepared me well for the unpredictable instability that being a working actress in Hollywood brought. You're hot one day, and *meh* not so hot the next. I went through some career droughts that really had me scared and shaken about my future as an actress. Age is not typically kind to women in my business as we constantly fight to reintroduce ourselves and be seen.

From early on, I wanted to be a news anchor or talk show host. For some obvious reasons, of course: I love to talk, I am curious as all hell, and I love to ask questions that I know others want to know the answers to. I adored watching Sally Jessy Raphael with her distinctive red glasses and marveled at how Ms. Oprah Winfrey moved about her stage and commanded the attention of the audience. She always seemed like she had the best job because she could spend time just chatting and asking questions to interesting people. That passion has never left me and has simmered in the back of my mind throughout my career. You could only imagine my surprise and thrill when I got the call to do a week-long audition in New York City for none other than the Emmy Award–winning talk show *The View*.

It was March 2015, and I was in Haiti doing charity work when my agent called to say *The View* wanted me to audition as a cohost for a full week because they were looking to fill the spot of Rosie O'Donnell, who had recently left the show. All I could think was, *Holy shit, this is a big opportunity!* I had been on the show a couple of times as a guest promoting whatever I was promoting, but to be in the running for a cohosting gig? This made my head spin! As always, I started to preplan my life and prepare for all of the hypothetical what ifs just in case I was actually offered the job. This was not just any old type of opportunity. I would have to move back to New York City. The only hurdle that gave me pause was that I had two young boys and my ex-husband Mike would not let me move them. An understandable stance, because he is also a really hands-on dad and very involved in the boys' day-to-day lives. I started plotting how I would navigate going back and forth every weekend to spend time with my kids so I could make this huge opportunity work for everyone. Trust me, I would not have made such a disruptive upheaval in my life for just any job, but this was *The View*! I loved the show, and this would literally be a dream come true for me. I worked out some sticky scheduling details with Mike, and he gladly made all the necessary accommodations to our schedules with the boys so I could be in New York for the upcoming week to audition.

I was thrilled, excited, and nervous as well. The first morning when I got on set all of my pent-up excitement quickly faded when I realized that my cohosts weren't quite as thrilled or welcoming as I thought they would have been. At the time, I was scheduled to work alongside Whoopi Goldberg, Nicolle Wallace, and Rosie Perez. I distinctly remember being alone in the wardrobe room with Nicolle and I said, "Oh, do you have kids?" Because I didn't really know her, I thought this was a good topic to initiate small talk and open up a dialogue.

Mind you, we were the only ones there getting wardrobe and she says, "Yeah." She didn't say, "How about you?" "Who are you?" "Nice having you here this week." Nothing. I took that curt answer as my cue to shut the hell up and mind my own business. I could be wrong but that was the vibe I was feeling. It didn't get any better as we all met up in the first top-of-the-morning meeting with producers. I was shocked and appalled to see how testy Whoopi was with the show's producers. I was embarrassed and disappointed, to say the least. It was cringeworthy! Here I was the eager new kid in class and I ran smack dab into the reality of an uninviting workplace. There was a brief nonchalant recognition that I was the cohost up to bat that week. No greetings or welcoming niceties, just a hey and they continued on with the meeting. Okay.

Now I was even more nervous. The initial vibe was all messed up, and it threw me off balance. We completed the first show, hit our marks, and I thought it went pretty well. It was hard to actually gauge my contribution because nobody really talked to me afterward or gave me any feedback. The ladies only really interacted, or talked to me, when we were cued up on set. The energy was cold, unfriendly, and standoffish. The atmosphere was so opposite to my friendly nature and definitely not what I had expected or hoped for. I had been on many different show sets in my time, and this experience was definitely a first. When I'm at someone else's show, as a rule I never close my dressing room door except if I'm actually changing clothes. My philosophy is that I am their guest and always want them to feel like I'm accessible and not "that diva behind the door." It was the second or third day into auditioning and my room door was ajar and I heard a knock on the open door. I was surprised to see Whoopi herself standing at the door. She said, "Hey!" I thought, *Oh, okay, this is a good sign, maybe we can finally sit down and have a nice chat and get to know each other.* The feeling of joy and hopefulness returned. She began by saying, "I was talking to my daughter and I was telling her who was here this week. She said she worked with you years ago."

"Oh ya, I remember that," I added.

"She said she remembered that you were the only person that was nice to her and actually spoke to her on set." She went on to share.

I was like, "Awesome. I liked her and we got along well. It was great working with her too." And just as quickly as she appeared, she disappeared back into the hallway without another word. Feeling good about making some kind of connection, I was optimistically looking forward to heading into shooting the next show. Because Whoopi was the lead, I thought our brief chat might change the dynamics and warm things up a bit. Nothing changed. N-o-t-h-i-n-g changed!

I felt like whatever I said got shot down and contradicted completely. I even decided to change my strategy and not give my opinions too quickly. I would just settle for piggybacking on whatever they said. That didn't work either. While we were filming and I was in the middle of making a point about something, I got a hard, firm kick under the table, by Rosie Perez, to shut me up. No, I'm not making this up nor being overly dramatic. It wasn't a kick like, "Oh, sorry, I was just crossing my legs" kind of jab. It was a shut-the-fuck-up-bitch, you're-talking-too-much signal kick!

After that show, I went back to my dressing room completely furious and disappointed by what had just happened. I told the story and shared my feelings of disillusionment with my glam team and they couldn't believe what they were hearing. I was shocked that a grown woman would act like that toward another grown woman, let alone in a professional setting! *Where the hell did I land? In the* Twilight Zone? *Was I being punked?* The day ended and I never got an apology for the kick from Rosie. The next morning, however, she came by my dressing room and knocked on my open door. "Hey, can I talk to you privately?" she asked.

I said, "Sure." My makeup artist quickly left the room to give us privacy.

She blurts out in her Brooklyn pitch, "Girl, you know, I just wanted you to know we needed you to be quiet. I thought you were gonna go on too long. You know, we have a system here and we know when the other one is about to talk. So I just wanted to stop you from talking too much." There, she said it. It wasn't just my imagination. I was dumbfounded. If there was a thought bubble floating above my head it would have said, *What kind of system is that where grown women kick each other like fucking mules? Was this a new type of Morse code or something? GTFOOH!*

All I could manage to get out of my mouth in my stunned state was, "Oh, okay." And she left the room. Still no "Sorry," but little did she know, she did confirm to me just how sorry she really was.

It was now Friday and the end of my week of auditions. I had lunch right after the show with one of the executives at ABC, and she was anxious and excited to hear my feedback on my time at *The View*. She was grinning enthusiastically and said, "So, what did you think? How was it?"

I paused and finally said pensively, "It's not for me." She looked at me in disbelief, like I had three heads. I think she was having a hard time processing what I said. And just like that, my wonderful dream of being a costar on *The View* went up in smoke. I went back home to California to be with my boys. I was so disappointed by the whole experience. Besides the fact that being a host of a talk show was a long-held wish of mine, I was also a diehard fan of the show and the women on it. The entire experience reminded me that sometimes you almost don't want to meet the people you admire because the reality of them might destroy your perception.

As a Black woman, I was so excited about working with Whoopi, who is such an icon of the acting world. She had made it against all odds and was acclaimed for her acting and philanthropy. To think, I could potentially share a stage with this giant among giants! What an honor . . . or so I thought. Listen, I'm a big girl and definitely nobody's shrinking violet. I can't say she wasn't just having a particularly bad week and I unwittingly got the shit end of the stick. Based on other people's experiences, I highly doubt it. But who knows? Admittedly, it was a crazy time when I auditioned for *The View*. There was so much uncertainty swirling around the show. Nobody knew who was losing their job and nobody knew who was leaving their job. Although I didn't become a cohost on *The View*, years later in 2021 I went on to star in a cyber-stalker movie, *Caught in His Web*, that Whoopi was executive-producing for the Lifetime network.

When I was approached in 2019 about joining the cast of The *Real Housewives of Beverly Hills (RHOBH)*, I didn't know what to think. On one hand, I was excited to work with my friends Denise Richards and Lisa Rinna, and this gave me comfort. On the other hand, I was nervous and full of apprehension about the scope of exposure this opportunity presented. Quite frankly, I was on the fence about it and leaning more toward taking a pass. It wasn't my genre, and I was nervous about putting my kids under that kind of scrutiny and spotlight. I tend to be a more private and "regular" type of person who relishes the fact that despite the occasional red carpet and fabulous party, I lead a pretty normal and quiet life. I guess you can say I enjoy the best of both worlds. I love going to the grocery store and shopping for myself. I look forward to joining my friends on weekend jaunts to local boutiques and restaurants. We go out to eat whenever and wherever we want, and people genuinely keep a respectful distance. Even when fans do approach me, it's just for a quick picture or comment, and then they go back to doing their business. I love my fans and am grateful they've connected with the body of work I've done. It's a huge honor for me to bring joy to and to touch the lives of people I don't know.

Of course, I had a heart-to-heart with Mike and the boys. Their input was crucial and would determine if I was actually going to commit. To be honest, Mike was hesitant at first because he wanted to make sure that the boys' lives were minimally impacted. We both agreed on that. They were smart and well-adjusted preteens, and I knew that I would protect them at all cost. I'd been careful to this point to be so protective of my kids and wanted them to enjoy a stress-free childhood away from the glare of the Hollywood gossip machine. Besides, I was thrilled to be able to be home more, traveling less, for them. The boys themselves were a little bit excited, but really could care less. Just another Tuesday afternoon to them. They were used to their mom being on camera. Nothing to see here, folks! I love them so much.

Another factor that had me tipping the scales in favor of a yes was Andy Cohen himself. I had met him randomly a few years prior at The Tower Bar, in the Sunset Tower Hotel in Hollywood, and we hit it off tremendously. I found him to be down to earth, smart, funny as hell, and extremely self-deprecating. My Spidey senses said that he was okay in my books; a really solid guy with integrity and class. My kind of people.

After inking the deal, the weight of the role crystallized and became enormous. Deciding to take on the role of the newest housewife meant that some of my privacy would go away. It also meant I would be representing Black women, Caribbean women, and my Haitian culture, and I did not take these roles lightly. Not only was I representing them to the world, I was also very aware that this was not your typical *Housewives* franchise. This was in the lofty 90210 zip code. The weight of the task ahead was heavy, and I was admittedly nervous and definitely apprehensive. This wasn't just a character I was being asked to play. This was pulling back the curtain on me being me. People were being invited to come into the sanctity of my home, see my kids up close and personal, and have a bird's-eye view of my personal life on display for public consumption. But, let's be real, this was also a huge platform that would enable me to reintroduce myself to my core fans. In a business sense, my goal was to broaden my audience and brand extension opportunities as well. The way I saw it, if I was going to join the *Housewives* franchise, this was probably the best place to land.

It was a calculated risk for me. As the first Black woman in the Beverly Hills franchise, I was confident that I would be able to have a little more control over my narrative. I couldn't imagine that the franchise would take the risk of trying to play out the mythical stereotype of the angry Black woman. If they wanted that, they wouldn't have come looking for me. More importantly, I wouldn't have agreed to compromise my brand and push that harmful narrative. Sorry, no amount of money or spotlight is worth that cost to me. I had painstakingly built a diverse and successful career before *Housewives* came along. I was already a model, working actress, author, producer, and businesswoman, and this was just another box to check. I had an established career as a successful actor that I was bringing to the table and I was proudly secure in that notion.

After the first season wrapped in December 2019, and I was able to see how it all played out, I was proud of how I had showed up. I think it depicted me pretty true to form. I am a fiercely loyal champion of my friends. Funny and full of energy. Definitely a hands-on mother who tries her best to make sure I'm present in my boys' lives and constantly looking for opportunities to teach real-life lessons. Optimistic, outspoken, spiritually in tune, searching for love, curious, and honest. Unquestionably honest!

Surprisingly enough, in my first season, I also made some really nice new connections and friendships. Enter Sutton Stracke, bless her heart. What does a well-bred southern girl and an inquisitive Haitian girl have in common? We don't know when to shut up and we say exactly what's on our mind—good, bad, or ugly! Have you seen us together? We really clicked and found a natural groove and kinship that made our freshman year a much easier experience. Sutton had never done reality television before and neither had I. Sutton had actually never even done TV, so she was in for an even bigger surprise than I was. Even though I had the television experience, I had to admit that reality TV was on a whole other level. We didn't know the rules, so we made up our own. I also loved how she showed up authentically. She owns who she is, and I appreciated that. Even when the cameras stopped rolling, Sutton is who I gravitated toward. She's kind, funny, quirky, and doesn't take herself too seriously. In short, she's my kind of gal.

Erika Jayne and Dorit Kemsley were also castmates I found camaraderie with, but for different reasons. With Erika, I took instantly to her no-nonsense, direct, cut-to-the-chase attitude. It was very New York. A little tough and dude-leaning, just like me. She's seen some things. I respected her story and struggle to get to where she was. Not an easy beginning, but she made it, baby! Dorit loved fashion just as much as I did; she's a girlie girl. She could put together a Chanel outfit as though it were a master class in Garanimals and I was here for all of it! Coming from the fashion world myself, I could tell this girl had an eye for style.

I must admit, by the end of the first season, I was a bit weary. Weary with the constant bickering back and forth about trivial things. "Your outfit is hideous" (that one came from me). "You wear too much makeup!" "[So-and-so] told me that you said this. . . ." I'm clearly paraphrasing, but that's what it sounded like to me at the end. Like Charlie Brown's teacher, "wah wa-wah wa-wah wa-wah wa-wah wa-wah wa-wah wa." I fully understood that controversy was always part of what made the series popular, but being on the inside was way more difficult than I anticipated. I guess part of it was that I was used to playing a character or a role for work. With this show I was showing up as myself and being judged on a personal level. It made a big difference and required a thicker layer of skin.

Nonetheless, if the season was difficult, the first reunion was torturous! I'm not going to lie; I felt attacked. It's one thing to watch it as a spectator, and another to be a target. I was caught off guard by how venomous these ladies, especially in this setting, could be. I had seen them claw and scratch at Denise Richards all season for something that she may, or may not, have done in her own private life. Denise had been a longtime friend of mine way before I decided to come on the show. We had known each other for more than twenty years and I trusted her and her character. Look, I'm not naive enough to vouch 100 percent for someone else's actions, not even a longtime friend's. It's also not my style to torture them over their personal decisions. At the end of the day, we are all grown people and allowed to do as we please.

One incident in particular that crossed the line and had me fuming came during a back-and-forth with Kyle Richards. I must officially state that I have nothing against Kyle and genuinely love her company and quirky spirit. She is a nice person, but even the sweetest of roses have their thorns.

It all began at Kyle's Children's Hospital Los Angeles charity event, which included a live auction bidding on a variety of prizes. Early on in the evening, I raised my paddle and bid on an all-inclusive Mexico vacation. I thought it would have been a great quick getaway for me and the boys. I bid; I won. I assumed they would get in touch with me later regarding the payment and that was the end of that . . . so I thought.

It's important to note that during my first season of actually filming *RHOBH* I was doing a tremendous amount of traveling across the country. I was simultaneously working on a variety of projects and wrapping up some prior commitments. I was also building, and moving into, a new home and managing all the details around that. It was a hectic time both personally and professionally. Fast forward to the first *RHOBH* reunion and we were all dressed to the nines, glittering and gleaming. I had on my beautiful yellow coat dress, carefully chosen because it was custom made by Jovana Louis Benoit, an up-and-coming Haitian fashion designer. Bold feathers on the cuffs, for added visual drama, and a majestic rhinestone headpiece to complete the regal look. I felt beautiful and ready to handle my business!

Boom, right out of the gate they started with me, and the jabs were flying. This was trial by fire. I mean, I've been put on the spot before, but this was different. I was fielding incoming fire from all angles. Then Kyle drops the atomic of all bombs, insinuating that I tried to stiff her and the charity for the Mexico vacation I bid on and won. If my head could have spun around on my shoulders, like Linda Blair in *The Exorcist*, it would have. Nobody calls me a liar—this is my biggest trigger! And you definitely don't call me a cheap and trifling liar who would stoop so low to stiff a charity. Fuck that! There are so many levels that this attack hurt me on, and I was stunned beyond belief that she wouldn't have addressed this with me privately. This was not cool. Over the years, I am proud that I have raised a lot of money for many charities, so I understand what donations mean to them and their cause. After the reunion was over, I was absolutely fuming and embarrassed. I immediately texted my business manager and discovered that no payment had been made to the charity. From my recollection, nobody from the organization had called me to even follow up or request payment either. I realize that Kyle didn't work for the charity herself, but she knew how to get in touch with me. She could have even forwarded them my contact information if there was a discrepancy in payment. I had also moved homes during that time period. Hell, she could have given me a heads up! In all the madness of the months after the event, it must have slipped through the cracks. I didn't even get a courtesy invoice sent to me about it. Either way, after I hung up the phone that afternoon with my business manager, payment was immediately forwarded. Done. Just like that, the issue was rectified. But now a new problem had reared its ugly head.

In my mind, Kyle must have known months in advance that payment wasn't yet submitted for my item. Instead of giving me the benefit of the doubt—perhaps a phone call, like most decent people would do—she saved the information and squirreled it away, plotting to weaponize it at the right time. And the reunion was just that time. That's the only explanation I see . . . there, I said it!

Little did Kyle know, but this type of obvious "snakery" wouldn't play well with audiences. Let me break it down from my point of view. These women have never had to deal with nor think of what it means to be Black in America. Not only are they white and have lived insulated in this world of privilege, they are also economically very advantaged. These inherent freedoms are taken for granted and they don't realize that people who don't look like them have to deal with a very different reality daily. Let's face it, some of the most hurtful stereotypes that Black people have had to battle against throughout history is that we are sneaky, can't be trusted, cheap, and shifty. Everything that woman just blatantly accused me of on international television. Yes, the *Housewives* franchise is seen in 170 different countries. She picked the wrong girl on the wrong day to do that to.

A few weeks later, Kyle called and asked to speak with me one-on-one to clear the air. We met up at a restaurant and she came in bearing gifts; nice touch. We started out with some harmless small talk. I could tell she was a bit nervous. She opened up the conversation by saying, "You know, I think we got off on the wrong foot. I felt like you didn't like me. You know, when I met you, I was so happy that you joined our group. I was excited. I liked you. I thought you were great." She went on, "And then at your LA Mission event where you were being honored you said, 'um, you know, and some not so much' when you were referring to whether or not you liked our *RHOBH* group."

I let her finish and said, "First of all, you were the only one that looked around and took my comment personally as if it was directed at you."

She continued, "Well, after you made the comment, Teddy said you looked right at me when you said it." My contention is I know I didn't look at anyone in particular when I made that joke during my acceptance speech. When I was onstage, the lights were so blinding that you weren't even able to focus on or see any one person. I really didn't mean for her, or anyone else, to take it personally. I was just playing it up a bit for the audience to get a laugh.

We went on to discuss and clear the air about some other trivial comments and incidents that got under her skin about me saying she was the least welcoming, how I called her outfit hideous, and how she felt slighted when I brought up her name during a *Watch What Happens Live* interview. I acknowledged her hurt and she apologized for making me not feel as welcomed during the first season of the show. There, the housekeeping portion of the conversation was over with. Now it was time to deal with the real heavy stuff. I asked her if we could fast forward to the reunion and brought up the incident of her attacking me about not paying my bill to the charity. I brought up how I felt about her not giving me the respect of calling me directly once she noticed the payment wasn't received. Her response was, "I don't take care of that. That's the charity. They are the people who collect the money. I don't do that." Listen, she wasn't getting off that easily because I know how that game works. I've hosted many charity events myself and I was technically her guest. The charity would have called her first.

I responded, "Well, Kyle, you know how to get in touch with me. You knew how to get in touch with me to pay for my portion of the five thousand masks we donated to hospitals earlier this year. We all paid for that. Why would I intentionally not pay for this?" I also pointed out that the charity event happened before we all went on the trip to Rome. I told her I was hurt to know she had this information and looked in my face the entire time during our trip and didn't once bring the issue up. I pointed out that she concealed, distorted, and weaponized an innocent misunderstanding and that's the conniving part.

Her response, "You know, when somebody comes after me, I have to fight back."

Then I broke down the darker, hidden implications to her. I told her that questioning my integrity ran deep for me because of who I am as a person. The second tier of hurt came because of the social and cultural stigmas attached to her accusations. I schooled her on the specific hurtful stereotypes historically assigned to Black people. She literally looked like a deer caught in headlights when I said that. Her eyes were darting back and forth. It looked like she was inwardly screaming to be rescued from our uncomfortable conversation. In the words of my friend Denise Richards, "BRAVO, BRAVO, F–KING BRAVO!" In that moment, my true purpose on the *RHOBH* journey manifested itself. In no way am I saying that Kyle is racist. I have never gotten that feeling from her, and that's not my intent. What I did realize through this process is that these women have never been forced to truly SEE people who looked like me, especially on their own level. She, like many others, has lived happily unaware. They've never had to listen to our plight. They've heard the talking points, but never truly took the time to listen. At that time, having that conversation, her eyes had been opened; she finally heard me.

To their credit, after my conversation in the restaurant with Kyle, the show's producers were grateful for my candor. I started, "I don't know if you guys were expecting me to flip a table, chuck water at her, or go ballistic?" I continued, "That's not my style and that's not who I am. I didn't want it to be a conversation filled with four-letter daggers. I wanted to genuinely share some insight with her that she might not have thought of. This was a serious matter for me. To me, the most powerful thing you can do is leave people with a little nugget of wisdom to chew on."

The producer said, "Garcelle, on this show we haven't had these types of conversations you had with Kyle today. It was perfect and so timely. These are the types of conversations everyone is having around the world right now. We would never have been able to have it so candidly if you weren't here. Thank you." This put my mind at ease and gave me comfort in knowing that in my own small way, which I never fully expected, I was making a historical difference.

The second season of *RHOBH* turned out to have its own set of spills and unexpected thrills. My longtime friend and partner-in-crime, Denise Richards, opted to bow out of the show suddenly. I can't say I really blamed her. She was taking low blows from all angles. Denise is still my dear friend and always will be. Reality TV didn't make us, and it sure can't break us! It was just her time to say ta-ta-for-now. In life, you've got to know when to hold 'em, know when to fold 'em! Thanks for that lesson, Kenny Rogers.

The newbies on the chopping block in the second season included the grande dame of 90210 herself, Kathy Hilton, big sister to Kyle Richards, and entrepreneur Crystal Kung Minkoff. Mixing the "traditional" Beverly Hills set with the new-school socialites proved to be a nice combination. Besides the status element, I really liked having another woman of color, an Asian sister, prominently recognized in the franchise. As I said before, representation matters. Kathy, however, proved to be one of the biggest surprises for me.

This chick was more fun than I could ever have imagined. She was kooky and self-deprecating, which was a charming surprise. I must confess, I imagined that Kathy would have entered the scene with a fabulous Birkin bag dangling from the crook of her arm, an ultrathin Virginia Slims teetering from perfectly manicured fingers, and a nose firmly pointed upward to sample only the very best air. Just saying the name Hilton, I instinctively add a little more base and refinement in my voice, forget all the other thoughts of grandeur that get conjured up. *Check yourself, Garcelle, stereotyping works both ways*. In reality, this lady was classy, funny, and really comfortable and easy to be around. Now that I had made amends with Kyle and the ice was broken, I could see the warm similarities between them. I liked Kathy instantly. Again, my type of gal. That's the thing about exposure to things outside one's usual comfort zone, it teaches you even when you don't think you have anything to learn. And that's the real "reality" of it all!

Nine

Prime-Time Adventures

Give a girl the right
pair of shoes and she can
conquer the world.

—Marilyn Monroe

n between television gigs, I've covered a lot of ground on the big
screen as well. *Coming to America* was my "cherry pop" moment and
has been the gift that keeps on giving throughout my professional
life. I even got to live out my fantasy of being a video vixen when I
appeared in Luther Vandross's music video *Take You Out*. Hey, who
could resist? It was Luther-hot-damn-Vandross! Let's just say I took
one for the team.

In the screenplay of my life, the small screen has proven fruitful as well. As a matter of fact, it's been the place where I've experimented the most with my acting style. *Miami Vice, Family Matters, The Fresh Prince of Bel-Air, The Jamie Foxx Show, NYPD Blue, Franklin & Bash, The Magicians, Chicago Med, Siren, Power, Tell Me a Story*, and *Carol's Second Act* under my belt. It's hard for me to tell you how I categorize my career.

I'm going to toot my own horn a bit here. Some pretty freaking major films have come my way as well. *Coming to America, Wild Wild West, Double Take, Bad Company, Barbershop 2: Back in Business, American Gun, Flight, White House Down, Small Time, Spider-Man: Homecoming*, and *Coming 2 America*. Because you know a little bit more about me by now, it will not be a surprise to you that I've always had a little issue with the industry term "leading man." That being said, I've worked with some pretty awesome, generous, and amazing men who have pushed me to grow and develop my acting skills. Eddie Murphy, Jamie Foxx, Garrett Morris, Will Smith, Anthony Hopkins, Chris Rock, Denzel Washington, Dennis Quaid, and Michael Keaton. That's a dream team lineup by anyone's standards, I would say.

Everyone always asks me what was it like filming *Coming to America* with such an amazing group of Black actors. For me, it was by far a more epic role and bigger than I even realized in my novice state. Even though my role in *Coming to America* as "rose bearer" was a small one, I made a lasting impact on the set. I ended up dating Eddie Murphy on and off for a year or so. Didn't see that one coming, did you? I even had the audacity to double-book a date with him once. I remember giving the sophomoric explanation that I had to end the date early because I had a "headache." To top it all off, as we pulled back up to my apartment, my other date was pulling up at the same time. I've never talked so fast or sweated so much in my life!

Eddie and I had some good times together. He was sweet and extremely charming. I absolutely adored his mother, Ms. Lillian. She was feisty, warm, and loved her son. In my opinion, I always felt like she really liked me, and if she could have chosen, she would have wanted us to end up together. I remember it was May 1993. I was married to Danny at the time when I saw Eddie and Nicole on the cover of *Ebony* magazine. They were gleefully announcing that they had gotten married and showing pictures of their fairy tale wedding. I knew that he had gotten married, but to see the happy couple in your face hit me harder than I expected. Danny was with me at the time and I guess my face showed my heartbreak. He was like, "What's wrong with you?" All I kept repeating in my head was, *Wow, she got him and I didn't!* I was devastated because I knew that he was such a good guy and I had fallen in love with him. In our relationship, timing and distance were our downfall. I was out there doing my thing, focused on trying to get my career off the ground. I lived in New York and he was bicoastal, so geographically, it was hard to keep it together and make it work. Who knows? He might have been the one that got away!

Speaking of weddings interrupted, I remember having to cut my honeymoon with Mike short because I had to shoot the movie *Bad Company*. I was married on a Saturday and left for Prague on the following Monday to shoot with legendary director Joel Schumacher, alongside Mr. Anthony Hopkins himself and funny man Chris Rock; not a bad consolation prize. We had a one-night "express wash" type of honeymoon!

Years later, I was reuniting with Jamie on *White House Down* and we had a blast. Oh, and fine-ass Channing Tatum was a bonus. Even though the movie didn't do well according to box office standards, it was like coming home for me. We had endless laughs and fell easily back into our comfortable camaraderie. He was the Black president and I was the Black First Lady. We had both come a long way from our early days at King's Tower on *The Jamie Foxx Show*. I was so proud to see how his career had flourished. When you've got talent like that in so many different buckets, it's bound to spill over in abundance.

Even when I was younger, I never really understood the girls who complained about modeling. I got to travel and see the world. I got paid a lot more than a seventeen-year-old would working at McDonald's. What's there to bitch about? I was really grateful. Being an immigrant and seeing the value in the opportunities in the United States also made me approach the world differently. I've always enthusiastically embraced the hard work that came along with it. People always tend to focus on the glory but gloss over the tedious work it takes to get to it. Knowing the dedication and commitment that went into the girl you see today has added to the sweetness of the rewards for me. As a friend of mine always likes to sarcastically remind me, at least we aren't out there digging ditches. Get over it!

I've never been afraid to try new things because they're different.

As such, I've been able to create longevity and relevance long after many believed them possible. Not one to wait around for things to happen to me, I frequently run headfirst into opportunity and pray I don't end up on my face. That's just my passion and drive coming together. An acting teacher once told me that, "You have to live life so you can play life."

I've never been a student at any fancy college or institution of higher learning, nor do I have any letters of accomplishment after my name. As a matter of fact, I didn't even graduate from high school, to be completely honest. Not that I don't believe wholeheartedly in higher education; that's just not where my path led me. I do, however, pride myself on being a quick study and a devout student of life.

I began feeling the itch to produce my own projects in my late forties. Much of what I've done in my career has been in front of a camera, but I never imagined that I had what it took to call the shots, create platforms and opportunities, and tell the stories I wanted to see myself in. Then, in 2017, I joined forces with a dynamo, young Emmy Award–winning producer Lisa L. Wilson, and Beauvais Wilson Productions was born. Oh, BTW, that middle *L* in her name is very important to my girl. I was finally going to take control of my "what's next?" on my own terms.

In 2018, Lisa and I took on our first project under the Beauvais Wilson Productions banner. The little twenty-five-minute film that changed our lives was called *Lalo's House*. Even though it was a small-budget independent film, it was a huge step in my evolution as a power broker and crafter of my own legacy. I was not only the lead actor—the villain, actually—I was the executive producer as well. With this project, I was driving the content, timing, and everything else like I had never done before with any of my roles or projects. It was prime time for sure!

A small, independent film documenting the horrors of child sex trafficking in Haiti, *Lalo's House* delved into the undercover and sinister dealings of a Catholic orphanage acting as cover for a child sex-trafficking ring. The harrowing tale unfolds after two sisters are abducted from their home in Jacamel, Haiti. I play the diabolical nun and headmistress of the school who orchestrates the operation. The story culminates in the sisters' fight to escape and shows the depths of destruction sex trafficking creates and leaves in its wake. An ambitious and heavy first story to take on, but one that needed to be told. Once I read the gut-wrenching script and realized it was based on a true story set in my home country, I couldn't look the other way. If not me, then who? In a weird way, the story found me.

The director, Kelley Kali, had been maneuvering for more than a year trying to figure out how we could connect so she could forward her script to me. Eventually, Kelley found a mutual acquaintance in Canadian film producer Marcel Jones, who connected us. She requested a meeting with me and we met up at the W Hollywood Hotel. There in the swanky decorated lounge, she passionately shared her story and journey of writing the screenplay with me. In 2010, she traveled to Haiti on a charitable mission after a major earthquake had crippled the country. During that mission, she had witnessed some questionable and discomforting things that she couldn't shake.

So when she made it back home to the United States, Kelley wrote the script as her thesis project for the film school at the University of Southern California (USC). Yes, this intuitive, passionate soul was a student at the time. To her parents I say, "Job well done!"

Instinctively, she said she had pictured me playing the part of the villain, Sister Francine, a twist she thought nobody would ever see coming. After completing the script, she then set out to turn her vision, including me, into reality. I had never played nor been offered a role like that before. The intricate details of the story and heartbreaking way she told it made me feel dirty, fortunate, and enraged all at the same time. How the hell could this happen in our modern-day society? These were children. Somebody's babies, for Christ's sake! They deserved a voice, safety, justice, and dignity. After our meeting, I was shaken to my core when I got back into my car and called Lisa. I immediately blurted out, "You have to read this script! We have to do it! We have to make this movie!" Soon after, Lisa and I signed on as executive producers and were superexcited to dig deeply into this project. This became a personal mission for us, way more than just work. We had initially floated the idea to a few trusted confidantes and they tried to dissuade us because they felt it was such a "heavy" story and topic to launch our production company with. Nevertheless, we listened to our instincts and started the process. Because of Kelley's link to USC, we got the school to let us take a crew of their students to Haiti to film the project. It was such a controversial and inflammatory subject that we couldn't even reveal the true nature of the story to the Haitian government at the time. After all, child sex trafficking was how some very influential and powerful people were making money. I also decided to bring Jax and Jaid on the adventure because I wanted to show them my home country and let them see their mom at work, even if I was taking on the most diabolical role I had ever played. I'm not going to lie; this added to the stress for me, but it was an exhilarating experience and one of my most loved projects to this day!

Not only was the project a personal triumph for me and my production company, it also got a tremendous amount of international buzz and acclaim. Kelley went on to win a Student Academy Award and a Directors Guild of America Student Film Award (DGA). *Lalo's House* went on to win critical acclaim from many film festivals as well. Besides all of the accolades the film got, one of the most important things to come out of this project is that it was instrumental in getting a human trafficking law changed in New York State. This was the little film that could. *Lalo's House* was small, but definitely mighty.

At about the same time, Marvel Cinematic Universe came calling, and I was honored to snag the role of Doris Toomes in *Spider-Man: Homecoming*. The film starred Tom Holland, Zendaya, Michael Keaton, and Robert Downey Jr., for God's sake. I mean, it's every kid's dream to be linked with a superhero. Playing this role gave me instant street cred with my boys. Even though I wasn't the biggest superhero fan myself, I knew enough to realize that this was more than just being part of a movie, it was being part of a movement! When Marvel calls, you answer, even if you don't know a dang thing about the characters. Whatever the role, I was signing on that dotted line!

Things came full circle again in 2020, during the pandemic, when *Coming 2 America* asked me to reprise my role as Rose Bearer Priestess. After thirty-five years, all the usual suspects were back on the scene. Even James Earl Jones was able to deliver another powerful performance as former king Jaffe Joffer of Zamunda. I gotta tell ya, this was such an affirming and validating moment for me. The buzz around it was so intense because the original was such a treasured piece of art in the Black culture. Even in the wider film-loving audience across demographic lines, *Coming to America* is a cult classic. Nobody wanted to mess with that mojo. I'm so glad they were able to bring on the powerhouse Academy Award–winning costume designer Ruth E. Carter. Not too shabby. . . . Talk about icons.

I have been lucky by anyone's standards. Actually, not lucky; blessed, to be more exact. I never take any of my relationships, successes, or windfalls for granted because I know that I didn't make it this far in Hollywood without a whole lot of help. Along the way, I've had agents and managers talking me down off many ledges and pushing me beyond my comfort level. PR teams boost me up and the understanding and support of my entire family who maybe didn't get as much one-on-one time with me as they needed. This is what it takes sometimes to chase your dreams and have them realized. It's behind the glaring studio lights, in the quiet sacrifices and unnamed support teams; that's where stardom really lies.

Ten

True Beauty

Some people are born
with a good eye,
or a good sense of smell.
I just know what speaks
to my soul.

—Garcelle Beauvais

Sophia Lauren, Elizabeth Taylor, Audrey Hepburn, Raquel Welch, and Bo Derek were the standards of beauty I grew up with. Although all were undeniable visions of beauty and sophistication, none of them looked like me, or anyone in my immediate circle. In the absence of these visual cues of acceptance, many women of color got the memo that we, and our likeness, were not desirable or acceptable. The heart-clenching stories I could tell of not seeing my own beauty as a little girl. I remember tightly wrapping towels around my head so they could playfully dangle down my back, all in the effort to pretend that I had cascading hair swinging and swooshing side to side like white girl's hair did . . . and mine didn't. Sadly, I'm not the only little Black girl who played these self-loathing games of make-believe.

Images of beauty we saw as little girls had a deeper and more sweeping effect on us as women, and especially women of color. Images, the words around them, and the frequency of them shaped the narrative we lived with. It seeped into every inch of our psyche, for better or for worse. Each time we saw the images, saw the joy, acceptance, and the implied lifestyle associated with them, it was like another nail in the coffin of our own self-esteem. Now to see it emulated, replicated, and duplicated in subtle and overt ways in "popular culture" was reaffirming. Even if we were bold enough to inwardly think we looked a little okay, it was never validated in any positive way. Black beauty was always beautiful; they knew it, we just never did.

Even though my journey started with my physical appearance, this ride has been way more than surface beauty for me. I was gutsy, and that was actually disarming and added to my charm. I didn't know what I didn't know, and acted as if I knew, if that makes sense. According to the laws of attraction, confidence creates an aura of beauty. In my case, it was that I was extremely curious and tenacious enough to seek answers, which passed itself off as confidence.

Today, as a grown woman who has been through some things, I know that to feel beautiful is to be beautiful. I've also come to learn that true beauty has little to do with outward appearances; that would be too easy and way too temporary. When I think of a beautiful woman, my mother, Marie Claire, immediately comes to mind. She was a queen to me. Regal and full of grace and poise. Her quiet strength, her resolve, her attention to detail when it came to taking care of herself. She taught me the beauty of appreciating the beauty in everything. "Always remember to look good, smell good, and taste good!" That's the little nugget of wisdom my wise mama shared with her daughters. I live by this mantra to this day. She taught us to hold ourselves to a high standard so that regardless of what comes our way, we always knew who we were and what our value was. Her strength was a thing of beauty. Mom was pure grace, and that's where her magic radiated from.

Feeling totally beautiful and comfortable in my own skin was a harder nut to crack for me. It's something that I grew into, as you now know. As Caribbean women, we are taught that buxom curves and fullness made you sexy. Then you entered America and the "real world," or in my case the modeling world, and all those ideas went out the window. Food became an enemy, whereas in my culture it was a symbol of love and a reason to gather and celebrate. Competing in a dimension where skinny was never skinny enough was counterintuitive. I was raised in my house to love the curve of my lips, hips, the slant of my nose, and everything else. In my case, it was because of my strong cultural and family foundation that I was able to remain somewhat tethered to, embracing my body at every stage. The struggles around being a Black model slightly blunted any perceived physical flaws and shortcomings I would have focused on. I didn't have time to focus on my waistline solely; I was a Black model in a white model's world.

As far as physical beauty and youthfulness go, I can't really take credit for them. As the saying goes, "Good Black don't crack!" I simply won the jackpot in the good genes category. I proudly admit that I have never been tucked, sucked, or poked in the cosmetic facial surgery sense. On top of it, I really don't have any complicated or intricate daily beauty routines that I adhere to either. I don't share this to brag, but this is the story of my sisters and many of my other Black girlfriends. Typically, I don't think an overwhelming majority of women in my culture obsess over antiaging prevention as much as other cultures, perhaps because we tend to age in a more forgiving way. Not all of us, but I think genetics definitely have something to do with it.

However, we all know that everyone has a different journey or definition of what it takes to be beautiful. I try not to judge anyone who chooses to go under the knife to enhance, or fix, what God gave them. To each their own, live and let live, as they say. I am terrified of ending up on the show *Botched*, which is part of the reason I don't love the idea of too much cosmetic surgery. Well, I must confess that in my twenties, I did have my breasts done. Call it societal pressure, call it restlessness, I thought it made me look "better." I didn't get them crazy porno big or anything, just a nice, believable "umph" size to add a bit more "s" to my curves. For whatever reason, at the time, I felt like bigger was the way to go, and now in my fifties, I've since had them removed. In a funny twist of irony, I think I've just outgrown the desire to have them. I'm going through my butterfly phase of metamorphosis. Kind of like when a snail doesn't fit its shell anymore, it leaves and seeks more comfortable housing. I outgrew those puppies, and it was time to move on!

If being crowned, in 2014, as one of *People* magazine's highly coveted Fifty Most Beautiful doesn't psych you out, nothing will. A funny thing about being in an industry ruled by beauty and perfection is that you often see that people's flaws are what tend to make them most beautiful. Most memorable for sure. The flaw is usually what makes someone stand out from the crowd and stand apart. The powers that be in Hollywood are waking up to this fact.

The phrase "feeling comfortable in my own skin" has always had a very different meaning for me. Suffering from extreme bouts of eczema has not been an easy road for me. Maintaining a "pleasing facade" is essentially part of how I've been able to make a living for myself. To call my system hypersensitive is an understatement. Looking at me you could probably never tell, but my skin is often on fire and enflamed due to the results of this condition. Agonizing irritation, itching, and bruising are side effects I've had to learn to live with. I have tried everything under the sun. Cleaner, mindful eating; minimal change. Countless cortisone shots for inflammation; only a temporary fix. Lotions, potions, and pills; the symptoms subside and only end up coming back. What makes it even worse is that my business, show business, is a mercilessly visual sport. This has made the struggle as much mental as it has been physical. Only recently have we been able to celebrate our individual flaws and own them as our badges of differentiation and unique beauty. Now, this is beautiful to me.

Born out of my own personal struggles with skin issues, one of the projects I'm working to get off the ground is a holistic skin care and beauty line for women of color. This venture is proof positive that from pain comes beauty. It was created because dealing with outward physical skin issues has taught me how difficult it is to find products that don't cause me to have a reaction. I also wanted to create beauty products for women with deeper skin tones. This will in no way be the first of its kind, but as with everything else, it's a numbers game.

Spiritual beauty is something I work on daily. It keeps me grounded and allows me to do the hard, continuous work of becoming the best version of myself. As I addressed earlier, a huge bundle of dried sage is never far from reach for me. It is a must have in my home. My life is full of hundreds of little decisions that need to be made. I know that my energy needs cleansing when I am wrestling with something and can't feel settled in my soul. When I find myself flip-flopping about something, I instantly recognize that it's my conscience and soul that are totally out of alignment. A quick meditation session, spark up a fat bushel of sage, a twirl around my house, and boom! Just like that, I feel instantly refocused.

Realizing the power of my own inner dialogue is a key part of maintaining my spiritual tranquility. The words we tell ourself in times of stillness and quiet manifest to the surface. Have you ever been around someone who's going through personal struggles and you can tell just by looking at them? In a lot of ways, true beauty lies in the energy we bring to every interaction. Being kind and forgiving to yourself helps you show up as your most beautiful self. Releasing the burden of perfection inevitably lightens the spirit. That's the golden ticket to beauty personified.

The sound of laughter is beautiful to me, and happy souls laugh often. If there is one memory that's burned in my mind it's that my mom's house was always filled with laughter. Even when times were tough, my mom would find reasons to smile and laugh. It's therapeutic. I loved to see her beautiful cheekbones rise and eyes twinkle with happiness. Even when I knew she was sad, she was still beautiful because I could feel her vulnerability and see her soul. The graceful way she lived her life reminds me that I can triumph through anything. To this day, even when I feel like crying, I sometimes just force myself to think of her and laugh. Not in a "get out the straitjacket" sort of way, but I just remind myself that there is beauty even in the struggle.

When I'm not laughing, I always try have a smile on my face. I'm big on giving out smiles for free. It costs me nothing and means everything. A simple smile can change attitudes, hearts, and minds. It is the greatest and most unexpected weapon a woman has in her tool belt. I can't tell you how many times I've gotten on an elevator full of strangers, flashed a smile, and said a simple greeting of hello and you would think I committed the worst crime. People usually do one of two things. They either smile back because it's contagious, or they look like someone just shot them and scowl uncomfortably. If you're a happy person, even if you're not in the happiest of places, you usually smile back.

Surrounding myself with beauty is what I like to do. For me, home represents peace, which leads to joy in my life. I love walking through my front door after a long, hectic day and feeling instantly relaxed and safe. Pretty and elegant decor in my home creates a solace for me. It's actually one of my secret weapons to creating my own joy. My Caribbean roots draw me to bold colors, patterns, flowers, and prints, which are all reflected in my own decor at home. Especially when I was decorating my new home, I chose soothing tones so I could easily integrate vibrant accents reflecting my personality. If you want to know how I get my weekly, sometimes daily, therapy on, ask my shopping crew. We have a ritual. We all hop in a truck, preferably an empty one with enough room in the back for whatever ends up in our carts. As soon as we get to the store, all bets are off. We immediately switch modes, putting on our game faces for the thrill of the hunt. I'm not playing; we take this sacred time very seriously. As soon as we enter the store, we each claim our own cart for the haul. Then we play follow-the-leader; usually we're following one friend in particular who is a stealth assassin at finding anything you need on the most obscure shelf. And she's short as hell too, so I don't know how she does it. She has a process that I must admit works well. We start at the front of the store and snake our way back and forth up and down the aisles. Why? Because we don't want to miss a single thing! I told you we were serious. Another little secret my friend taught me: We never leave a "maybe item" behind. Everything goes in the cart. and we can decide later. Just so nobody else snatches it up behind us.

We "ooh" and "ahh," giggling and touching our way through the store, all while discussing various topics, or things we need to get off our chest. It's magic. It works. You name it, we find it. Candles, serving trays, wicker baskets, towels, furniture, lamps, and pillows galore! There's something about shopping for beautiful home accessories that inspires my soul. Perhaps it's the carefree quality time spent with my girls too. This seemingly frivolous excursion actually allows me time to decompress. It truly makes everything better, I think. Then, when we finally schlep our trinkets home, set them in place, we gleefully marvel all over again, preferably over glasses of wine, at how much of a sanctuary they create. Home is where the heart is . . . mine always has to be beautiful and filled with loving energy!

The smell of fresh gardenias, or the deep love and connection I feel toward butterflies are physical reminders of that loving energy in my life. Any kind of butterfly. Their shape, form, and movement all represent the epitome of beauty for me. So is their commitment to the journey and struggle to get to their ultimate form. It speaks to my soul. My mother loved everything about butterflies as well; that's probably where I get my appreciation from. Everything about what a butterfly ultimately becomes centers around the notion that with struggle comes beauty. That's the story of women. The caterpillar knows instinctively when it needs to pull back and make itself small to fit into its cocoon. They naturally know when it's time to be still and quiet so they can go inward to grow. A beautifully simple concept and metaphor for life. The layers necessary for their evolution represent me and my journey.

Just like those colorful showy butterflies, I embrace beautiful fashion and color wholeheartedly. As I've often said, I think everybody looks better in clothes. In life, there are fashion lovers and fashion addicts. I fall into the latter category, and it's a drug I can't quit! Shoes have always been my soft spot, but I am pretty much mush in all other categories as well. Bright colors, bold prints, and unique tailoring and elements all have my heart. Dressing up and having freedom to experiment with such a wide variety of looks is one of the best parts of being a woman. I've also had the pleasure to work closely with amazing design professionals, from whom I've gotten a first-class, front-row fashion education. It's one of the perks of my job I enjoy the most. The thrill of the hunt, wearing one-of-a-kind pieces, and shopping right off the rack; I enjoy it all! I know they say that clothes don't make the person, but they sure do make this girl perk up. Contrary to Hollywood norms, I almost always style myself for red-carpet events, with help from my trusty assistant and friend Tazz. Some people have an eye for art, a finely tuned palate, or a sense of smell. I instinctively know what works for my body and silhouette. That's one of my secret superpowers!

To always fit into this wonderful wardrobe of mine is another thing. Regular organized exercise is a goal that often eludes me. Not because I don't love the invigorating and rewarding feeling of breaking a good sweat; I love that feeling. I love the thought of checking a good daily workout off of my to-do list. Unfortunately, like countless women, I love the idea of sleeping in an extra half hour, laying in bed and staring at the ceiling, lounging after a long day and just collecting my thoughts . . . anything but exercise! I own it and try and do better because I know that the physical discipline of exercise helps with my mental clarity and keeps me looking my best.

Eleven

Note to Self

You never find yourself
until you face the truth.

—Pearl Bailey

f I could talk to my five-year-old self, I would tell her YOU are enough. You always have been. Even with painfully skinny legs and protruding shoulder blades, an absentee father, a disjointed and hectic childhood, you've always been enough. Through two un-successful marriages, disappointing relationships, and yes, trou-bled years raising children, you've always triumphed. What you have brought to this universe has been perfectly imperfect but still always enough.

Deep within, you have never doubted that you had what it took to get to where you are sitting today. I have heard all the private conversations you have had with yourself. Saw all your wildly imaginative visions of grandeur. Listened to you cry yourself to sleep at night and saw you fall to your knees in a surrendered prayer of gratitude, and at times, hopelessness and despair. I've heard and seen it all, but still I believed in you. Believed in what you were raised to be. What you envisioned you were and, more importantly, what others said you could never be.

It has been a wild, exhilarating journey for us, and I know the best is yet to come. We've learned a lot about ourself and the world along the way. We've shrunken ourself and expanded our boundaries when we've needed and definitely proven our flexibility. Proven our value. All while keeping our eyes firmly fixed on the goal of longevity. Setbacks, stumbles, and falls be damned. This has always been a marathon and not a sprint for us. Others have passed us by. Even looped us many times in our long patchwork career. We've missed out on opportunities and been denied our just due, but here we are still standing. Flourishing beyond your wildest dreams, exploring, and striving in spite of it all.

You've masterfully figured out how to continually honor yourself, your faith, family, and friends in a business and in a world that constantly challenges your ability to do so. You have held steadfast to your beliefs and never strayed from who you are at your core; just Gachou. You've raised three wonderfully well-adjusted young boys into responsible young men all while maintaining your youthful spirit and hopeful glow. Remember to remind yourself that you've accomplished this remarkable feat all without the historical reference of a strong male father figure of your own. It's okay to admit to yourself that this, my dear, *is* a job well done.

You have slayed many dragons of lack and loss in your lifetime while wrestling with the nagging inner voice of self-doubt. Sometimes that nagging voice is so quiet and other times it's debilitatingly loud. Sometimes you win that battle, and other times you lose it. Yet still you've found your way to a place of forgiveness. For others and for yourself. Where did you find that strength to push forward? How did you develop that grit? Oh, that's right, I remember. You saw it in the loving eyes and selfless deeds of your single mother, KeKe. She would burst with pride if she could see all that you have accomplished today . . . somehow, I think she's still there by your side watching and encouraging you every step of the way. You found that compassion in the warm embrace of your older sisters Yves-Rose, Carole, Gladys, and Chantal, who helped carry you toward your destiny when you were younger—you modeled them. We honor them and thank them always.

To this day, you continue to surround yourself with a strong village of supportive women who lift each other up, cheer each other on, and carry each other's water when needed. Each and every one in your carefully curated circle of friends is your rock. They are your biggest fans, your harshest critiques, and your fiercest defenders. You know they have your back, and you, in turn, have theirs. You keep each other grounded, honest, and true. They allow you to be you without having to explain yourself.

Your ability to love and believe in love is remarkable. You continue to be an eternal optimist and this is what truly makes you a beautiful unicorn. It's actually contagious to all who enter your life. Through it all, you have never given up on chasing love, finding love, and nurturing love. This is who you are at your core. You protect your heart at all costs but are not afraid to give it to those who've earned it. Never let anyone else tell you who you are—you've done too much hard work figuring that out on your own. Be cautious of those who want to tear you down for their own ascension, or because of their own insecurities. You should never have to dim your own light to please anyone else. A light like yours is rare. Continue to narrate your own life story as well; you've been a very compelling storyteller thus far. You are fearless and fragile at the same time. You consistently wear your big heart on your sleeve. Sometimes it will work for you and sometimes it will work against you. Even though you are sensitive, I fear for anyone who crosses you. You are a skillfully sharpened double-edged sword standing at the ready. You've beautifully perfected the art of killing them with kindness while plotting your rise. Your kindness should never be mistaken for weakness.

You are compassionate, kind, and endlessly giving of your resources and time. You make others better without feeling like it depletes who you are. This is a wonderful gift to humanity. Cherish it. Nurture it, and continue to spread it. And, remember dear heart, to always live fully in your truth every chance you get. Drink it in, celebrate it, honor it. Most of all, believe it. Take comfort in knowing that your truth was fashioned based on real and painful experiences that you've triumphed over. Experiences that you learned from.

Experiences that would have broken many others. You never have to apologize for acting on the knowledge you've gained. We are gatherers of wisdom when it's all said and done. That's what we were put here to do. The truth shall set you free and bring you peace; even if it stings a bit at first. You envision the world in all its beauty and never miss an opportunity to help transform this ideal into a reality. You must realize that you can't be all things to all people at all times. Be content knowing that sometimes your best effort is all you can give. The simple truth is, you weren't put here to *be* the world, you were put here to help the world be better. And that is enough.

Your style and attention to detail are endless. You come from good stock. You take joy in beautiful things and you love every minute of being a woman. Your eyes light up with joy at the simplest and silliest of things. Laughter is your favorite form of medicine. You are such a kid at heart. Don't beat yourself up too much about your weakness for shopping; you've more than earned the right to this little luxury. YOU ARE BLESSED!

So continue to pick yourself up. Dust yourself off and keep up the good fight, baby girl. You have been, *are*, and will continue to be enough just as you are.

With love,

Garcelle's Gems

How did they carry so much and make it look so effortless? Isn't this the question we usually ask when we talk about a woman's burdens?

I am a woman who is proud
of her success but hasn't
completely bought into it.
A woman who enjoys the finer
things in life but hasn't accepted
the embarrassment of riches
associated with celebrity.

I have learned that shame is only
felt when you haven't unpacked
the heavy baggage you carry.
When you haven't admitted
that you are human and
allowed to falter.

Happiness must first come from within. It's meant to be shared and enhanced, not generated— especially if it's authentic joy.

I am not looking for someone
to complete me, either; I'm
learning how to fill in all of the
gaps myself and appreciate
the negative spaces.

Not only did my infertility teach me patience and resilience, through the process, I also had to reinvent the way I saw my body, motherhood, and pregnancy in general.

My mother was not a perfect
woman, and neither am I.
As a mother myself, I now
realize that staying on that
pedestal your kids put you
on is a shaky foundation
you're guaranteed to take
a tumble from. It's not only
guaranteed, it's healthy.

Sometimes you forget how strong you can be until you are put in a situation where you have to carry yourself.

I feel that we were given intuition to help guide us. Especially when knowledge and experience are lacking.

For me, friendship without intentional participation is just lip service. Anyone who really knows me can attest, I've never been one to do fillers—of ANY kind!

Mind your business, Garcelle,
mind your business.

Sometimes you almost don't want
to meet the people you admire
because the reality of them
might destroy your perception.

I think everybody looks better in clothes. Besides, women usually want to get skinny for other women, but men actually want something they can hold on to.

Others have passed us by.
Even looped us many times in our
long patchwork career. We've
missed out on opportunities
and been denied our just due,
but here we are still standing.
Flourishing, exploring, and
striving in spite of it all.

The simple truth is, you weren't put here to be the world, you were put here to help the world be better. And that is enough.

Acknowledgments

I couldn't end this book without saying a thank you to my ex-husbands. Don't be surprised. We're still all family who support each other in a variety of ways. I say thank you to Danny for being present and supportive, as both dad and grandfather, in Oliver's life today. The memories you are making are priceless. To Mike, I say thank you for always being an engaged, supportive, and hands-on dad to our twins, Jax and Jaid, and Oliver as well. After all, redemption is not only reserved for me; we all can achieve it.

And because nobody achieves success all by themselves, I must thank the following who have been with me on varying legs of my journey. Some carrying me, some pushing me, some covering for me, some drying my tears, teaching me, cheering for me from the sidelines, and others propping me up after a long day; I thank you all for playing a starring role in my life!

Book team: Amistad (Judith Curr and Patrik Henry Bass, you created a space where I felt safe and free to show the world the complete version of me); Park & Fine (Celeste Fine and Sarah Passick, for

Acknowledgments

recognizing that if not now, when?); Nicole E. Smith, my coauthor and bestie (thanks for doing double duty, my sister from another mister. We did it!).

Family: My brothers Maurice and Elie; my sisters Yves-Rose, Carole, Gladys along with her husband, Carlo Casimir, and Chantal. Also, Marie-Flore Beaubien, Natasha DesRuisseaux, Danny Saunders, Mike Nilon, Jack and Rita Nilon, Stephanie and Joe Decker, Vashni Perkins, Lucy Bell, and Samantha Saunders who blessed me with baby OJ, my first grandson. And last but not least, our crazy one-eyed dog Bear.

Business teams: Gordon Gilbertson, Steve Muller, Babette Perry, Mark A. Johnson, Esq., Mona Loring, Neal Marks, CPA, Becca Paredes, Lori Sale, Tenia Watson, and Lauren Blincoe.

My Hollywood "families": Innovative, MGM Studios, Barry Poznick, Evolution Media, *The Real Housewives of Beverly Hills*, *The Real*, *Hollywood Today Live*, Beauvais Wilson Productions, Los Angeles Mission, Howard Fine Acting Studio, The Groundlings Theatre & School, Tim Taylor, Ford Models, and Irene Marie Models.

Dear friends: Glynis Costin, Lisa L. Wilson, Tahiese "Tazz" Beckford, Jonaura Wisdom, Heather Russell, Kim Kimble, Robear Landeros, Julie Jules, Jamie Foxx, Andy Cohen ("Bravo Bravo Bravo"), Sherri Shepherd, Sheree Zampino, Nischelle Turner, Christos Garkinos, Rwaana Brooks "Tex," Anastasia, Taraji P. Henson, Laili Ali, Sarah

Acknowledgments

Michelle Gellar, Denise Richards, Liz Dennery, Andy Parker and Michael Birnbaum, Natalie Macaulay, Asa Soltan Rahmati, Angela Bassett, Ali Landry, Angie Harmon, Judith Joseph, Carole Philips, Jill Marie Jones, Jennifer Marquet, Halle Berry, Erick Robinson, Whitney Pavlik, Claudine Oriol, Dania Ramirez, Josh William, Calvin Hughes, Kym Nicole Oubre, Carson Kressley, Ted Bunch, Suzanne Lerner, Arsenio Hall, Eddie Murphy, Dondré Whitfield and his wife Salli Richardson-Whitfield, and Jawn Murray.

Credits and Permissions

All photos courtesy of Garcelle Beauvais unless otherwise noted.

Insert, page 6, bottom right: Johnny Louis / JLN Photography

Insert, page 7, top right: © Michael Caulfield / Wire Image/ Getty Images

Insert, page 9, top right: Tonya Wise / Associated Press

Insert, page 9, bottom right: © J. Vespa / Getty Images

Insert, page 10, top left and right: Ford Models

Insert, page 10, bottom right: *Essence Magazine*

Insert, page 11, top left and right: Playboy Inc.

Insert, page 11, bottom left: *People Magazine*

Insert, page 12, top left: *People Magazine*

Insert, page 13, top right: Beauvais Wilson Productions

Insert, page 13, bottom left: Beauvais Wilson Productions

Insert, page 13, bottom right: Beauvais Wilson Productions

Insert, page 14, top: © Getty Images

Insert, page 15, top: Bros. Unscripted Television / Telepictures Productions

About the Author

Named one of *People* magazine's highly coveted "50 Most Beautiful," Haitian-born actress Garcelle Beauvais immigrated to the United States at the age of seven with her mother and sisters, and has since charmed audiences with her dramatic and comedic abilities. Balancing perfectly between the small screen and big screen, she proudly became the first Black cast member on Bravo's *The Real Housewives of Beverly Hills* (April 2020). She has been busy working on her podcast titled *Going to Bed with Garcelle*, a fun and flirty late-night podcast featuring no holds-barred girl talk on sex, life, dating, and relationships. This past year, she also joined Fox's multi-award-winning talk show *The Real* as the new co-host (September 2020).

A look back at Garcelle's career shows a hybrid of businesswoman and mother who has been a cherished face in Hollywood for more than three decades. She got her start in nineties comedies *The Fresh Prince of Bel-Air* and *The Jamie Foxx Show*. She went on to appear in television on series such as SyFy's *The Magicians*, NBC's *Chicago Med*, *NYPD Blue*, *Franklin & Bash*, HBO's *Curb Your Enthusiasm*, *Arrested Development*, *Power* on Starz, and many others. On the voice-over side of work, Garcelle was heard in the Nickelodeon

About the Author

mini-series *Middle School Moguls* as "Mrs. Pierre" in her native Haitian accent.

Film has always been a passion for Garcelle. She has starred in box office hits *White House Down* with Jamie Foxx and Channing Tatum as the First Lady of the United States, *Flight* with Denzel Washington, *American Gun* with Forrest Whitaker, *Coming to America* (1988) and the sequel *Coming 2 America* (2021), where she worked once again with Eddie Murphy, *Bad Company* with Chris Rock, *Barbershop 2: Back in Business* with Queen Latifah, and *Spider-Man: Homecoming* with Tom Holland, among others.

Above all, Garcelle's most important job is being a mother. She was inspired by motherhood to write a children's book series entitled *I AM*, addressing identity issues relevant to many children today. There are three successful books in the series.

Garcelle supports the Step Up Women's Network, a national nonprofit that empowers women and girls to be strong and reach their full potential. She is also an active supporter of UNICEF and Angels for Humanity, an organization that helps children in Haiti through education and health-based initiatives.

She resides in Los Angeles and has three sons—Oliver, her first, and twins, Jax and Jaid.